The Memory Pool

THERESE SPRUHAN has a passion for swimming pools. She writes about them on her blog *Swimming Pool Stories* and shares photos on Instagram @swimmingpoolstories. She has published articles on places to swim in the *Weekend Australian* and contributed words and photos to *The Pool*, Australia's exhibition at the 2016 Venice Architecture Biennale, re-exhibited at the National Gallery of Victoria in 2017–18. She lives in Sydney with her husband Bruce and is a regular swimmer at her local pools in Petersham, Leichhardt and Enmore.

The Memory Pool

Australian
stories of
summer, sun
and
swimming

Therese Spruhan

NEWSOUTH

A NewSouth book

Published by
NewSouth Publishing
University of New South Wales Press Ltd
University of New South Wales
Sydney New South Wales 2052
AUSTRALIA
newsouthpublishing.com

© Therese Spruhan 2019
First published 2019

10 9 8 7 6 5 4 3 2 1

A catalogue record for this book is available from the National Library of Australia

ISBNs   9781742236582 (paperback)
         9781742244655 (ebook)
         9781742249148 (ePDF)

Design Josephine Pajor-Markus
Cover design Sandy Cull, gogoGingko
Cover image Little girl in swimming costume jumping, photograph by Michelle Livingston. *Arcangel*
Printer Griffin Press

All reasonable efforts were taken to obtain permission to use copyright material reproduced in this book, but in some cases copyright could not be traced. The author welcomes information in this regard.

This book is printed on paper using fibre supplied from plantation or sustainably managed forests.

UNSW
SYDNEY

Contents

Historic pools

Champions of the pool

Country pools

Introduction

Since the early 1960s, when I first met Northbridge Baths, a tidal pool in a quiet corner of Sydney's Middle Harbour, I have been hooked, in love with swimming pools. That love has continued throughout my adult life and, over the years, I've formed close relationships with several local pools. But my strongest bond will always be with that first pool at Northbridge, a place that was like my best friend when I was a child.

I've always known I wasn't alone in my affection for a childhood pool, and when the idea for this book started swimming around in my head, similar tales of deep connection started to surface – in the books and articles I was reading, in interviews on the radio, in conversations and in my travels to pools in places across the country from Darwin to Lightning Ridge and south to Launceston.

All those 'memory pool' leads went into a file, and then I started trying to contact people I knew – or had a hunch – had a close connection to a childhood pool. With the philosophy of 'nothing ventured, nothing gained', I sent hopeful emails and messages to literary agents, managers and social media accounts. I turned up at book and CD launches and writers' festivals, and even bailed up one potential interviewee when I spotted her in a Sydney shopping centre.

When I explained the idea for the book, most people had an immediate connection and straight away wanted to be part of *The Memory Pool*. My next step was to interview each person and find out why the pool was so much more to them than a place to cool off in summer. I asked about their first meeting with 'their pool', about special memories, favourite spots, and what that watery place meant to them as a child.

Once the interview was transcribed, I wrote each person's story as if they were telling it to the reader themselves; I wanted the distinctive voice and experience of each to come through. The result is 28 stories celebrating the pool by Australians aged 28 to 97 from all over the country, and from a range of different aquatic settings – chlorine, sea, bay, river and backyard.

The stories take a dive deep into the inner world of the pool, a place of daring, competition, belonging, solitude, fantasy, freedom, friendship, escape, sex and love. There are common threads of learning to swim, warm concrete, hot chips and chlorine, bombs and the brush of skin on skin. There are also many examples of how a simple structure like the local pool could inspire imaginations, build courage, fulfil dreams and provide refuge.

A big thank you to the 27 people in this book for sharing their precious memories with me. It has been exciting connecting with so many people across Australia who have such wonderful recollections of a childhood pool.

I hope you enjoy dipping into their stories, and mine, in *The Memory Pool* and when I say, *On your mark, get set, go!* – prepare to dive in.

Therese Spruhan
Sydney

Suburban pools

TRENT DALTON

Sprinting to the Sandgate swimming pool

In 1985, when Trent Dalton's single mother fell on the hardest of times, he moved from the south side of Brisbane to the north. Initially he and his three older brothers lived with their paternal grandparents in Sandgate, then with their father in his Housing Commission home at nearby Bracken Ridge. When Trent was six, he discovered the Sandgate swimming pool, a place that became his summer sanctuary for the next 12 years of his life.

The first time my brothers and I went to the Sandgate swimming pool, our journey started from our grandparents' house in Deagon Street, Sandgate. My dad's dad, Vic, was this outrageously heroic man, a former Rat of Tobruk who lost his leg in north Africa in World War II. My grandmother Beryl had had polio and she got around in a wheelchair. One day my granddad and a bunch of wonderful local people built Nan this long ramp that went for about 15 metres from the front door of their two-storey house all the way to the footpath. That ramp is vivid in my mind because my brothers and I would sprint down it, out the front gate, down the footpath and then run the whole darn way to the Sandgate swimming pool. The bitumen was always hot on our bare feet and we'd run along the grass as much as we could.

If our old man gave us a lift to the pool, my distinct memory is of being on the hot vinyl seats with my brothers in the back of his sky-blue Holden Kingswood early on a Saturday or a Sunday morning. We'd be giddy with excitement and we'd roll around in the back of that car with no seatbelts and we'd scream this mantra from a scene in the *Star Wars* movie: '*Almost there, almost there!*' They were the words of the pilot at the end of the *Star Wars* battle when he's trying to drop a bomb into the Death Star and he's saying back to the base, 'Almost there, almost hitting the target.' We'd say it incessantly in an American voice and we'd let that mantra build till it peaked to this crescendo and the old man, Noel, would yell, 'Shut up. Yes, we are almost there!' And then there was this release when we reached the Sandgate swimming pool, which was in the most amazing location on the beachfront. And we would scream, '*Made it!*'

I don't even know if we had t-shirts or if we were in anything but bare feet, shorts and a towel over our shoulders. We'd pile out of the car and run to this amazing place, the Sandgate swimming pool, which had these strange brown turnstiles with metal horizontal bars. You had to go through them one by one and that process of pushing through those turnstiles was going from one world to another. It was like Dorothy in *The Wizard of Oz* going from black and white into colour – into technicolour. Moving from the outside of Sandgate pool to the inside meant we arrived into a whole other wonderful universe that meant so much to all us Dalton boys – Joel, Ben, Jesse and me. It was our sanctuary.

Once we were inside we'd chuck a left and run across the hot concrete beside the big swimming pool. We sprinted everywhere when we were kids and at that pool we sprinted to the top of this massive grassy hill, which probably wasn't that massive but to me as a six-year-old it was steep. We'd lay our towels down and then we'd wait for all the brothers to be ready and then line up like a race and say, 'Are you ready, are you ready?' and then, '*Go!*' We'd sprint down that grassy hill and some of us would trip and tumble and graze our knees and not quite make the pool. But if we kept our balance as we were going down and onto the flat then we'd make it to the pool.

The water inside that pool was like an oasis of cool after all our running and the hot Kingswood, and high summer in Brisbane was hot. We are talking sweaty, humid 36 degrees. We'd be laughing ourselves silly by the time we splashed into the pool. Invariably our eyes got burnt to hell because the muscle-bound manager knew that every kid in the northside of Brisbane was about to hit that pool, so to accommodate all those germs he put so much chlorine in. We usually got there really early and that first-thing-Saturday-morning chlorine would hit our eyes and we would be dealing with the pain of it for the rest of the day. That pain would still be there that night when we were watching the one-day cricket, Australia vs West Indies, and we'd still be rubbing our eyes from the chlorine. But we'd take that pain any day from the Sandgate swimming pool because the place was magic.

The muscle-bound guy who loaded in all the chlorine was part of a family who ran the pool. They were all blond-haired and tanned and he looked like Arnie Schwarzenegger. He'd won prizes for bodybuilding and when he wasn't pumping iron he did all the maintenance around the pool. He was actually the sweetest guy and never threw his weight around, but you'd never mess with him or give backchat at the canteen. He spoke in brief sentences and you'd grab your hotdog, popcorn, Calippo or slush puppy from this giant hand, which made all the food look like little Lego pieces. He'd hand over this stuff and you'd go, 'Thank you,' and dream of one day having muscles like his. He was a legend with my mates and when you saw him around Sandgate you knew summer was here. If you saw him at the shops you'd nod to him and point him out to your dad.

My journey as a swimmer at the Sandgate swimming pool was a classic. I didn't know how to swim when I first went there, but my three older brothers did. The way Sandgate pool was laid out, there was this senior 50-metre pool and then there was a lagoon-shaped wading pool with a white concrete bridge that split the wading pool from the intermediate pool. After we'd done our run down the hill, my brothers went straight into the intermediate pool and I went into the wading pool. I wanted to follow my brothers into the intermediate pool, but to get into that pool you had to be able to swim.

One day, in the space of 20 minutes, it was either drown or swim. My brothers were telling me, 'You can do it,' as I was splashing around and drowning and then I started flapping my arms about and then I swam. I don't know whether the great Laurie Lawrence, who has taught more kids in Queensland to swim than anybody on the planet, would endorse that way of learning to swim, but I think he is a believer in just getting in and doing your best and going for it. And that is probably the way a lot of Queensland kids learned to swim.

It was my ambition to hang out with my brothers that made me determined to learn to swim. When I was eight or nine, my swimming was good enough to start having a go in the senior pool – diving down trying to touch the bottom of the deep end and doing bombs off the blocks that sometimes you'd get in trouble for because you'd nearly land on top of someone swimming laps. We still liked the intermediate pool and some days we'd hang in there and do backward somersaults underwater.

One day I was sitting on the edge of that pool dangling my legs in the water. I was looking up at the sky and dreaming away, something I did all the time, and suddenly these arms were around my neck. Big sweaty arms. I was probably about eight years old and I was immediately frightened. I thought this kid was attacking me. I was yell-ing, '*F– off, f– off!*' and was pushing him away. I was really angry with this kid, who was older than me but I could tell he wasn't like me. And then his mum came running up and said, 'It's all right, he's just trying to hug you.'

Then I started crying because I was so sad for the kid because of the way I had reacted. I hadn't come across any people with Down Syndrome then and I couldn't express how sorry I was. His mum kept saying, 'It's all right.' Then the kid was smiling at me too. And the love in that kid's face, I swear to God it made me cry. It was so warm and I just loved that kid so much immediately. I wasn't getting a lot of hugs back in those days and this kid had wanted to hug me. He just randomly thought that I was a kid that he might want to hug and then play with in this pool. He had the same excitement about the Sandgate swimming pool that I had and he was saying, *Isn't this the best?* When I look back, it was a beautiful moment in my life about perspective and how you can read things wrong.

There were many profound moments at the Sand-gate swimming pool through those years from when I was six till 18. You'd have a fist fight in the pool and you'd find your courage. If older kids came up to you and tried to take your Calippo, in that moment you showed your strength. There were all those sorts of things that hap-pened throughout a 10-hour day that shaped you. The feeling in your heart when some girl looked your way and you realised that girls are these magnificent creatures and suddenly you understood that they might be a very big part of your life. From about six till about 13 you weren't interested in them at all but then things unfolded in that glorious setting.

There were awakenings and one of those was Aleta Green. Aleta Green went to Nashville State High School where I went, and she was the girl that every fella loved. She was pretty spectacular to any 14-year-old boy at that time and one day she emerged from the pool in this new purple bikini. It was a lavender colour which I'd never seen before and the way she wore that bikini we realised that she was a woman and we were boys. She was so far beyond us. But that slow-motion moment is tattooed on my brain. It's forever there. It went down in history and my mates would talk about it till we were 18, till we were 25 and we all became dads.

It was pretty simple that pool – a massive dugout filled with chlorinated water – but what made it magical was you could do so much within it. You could duck your head underwater and kiss a girl, you could scream things to your mate underwater and try and get him to translate. You could float on top of the water for hours and day-dream or you could execute a backflip and find out how brave you were and see how many flips you could pull off. You could see how long you could stay underwater and how much endurance you had by the number of laps of the pool you could swim. You could discover so much in that one simple thing, the swimming pool.

I'd spend hours in the water and then I'd go back

to my towel and lie in the sun and just daydream, lost in thought, and then invariably one of my mates would come over and their head would block the sun and they'd say, 'Trent, Trent – what are you staring at?' I'm not staring at anything. I'm staring into another universe and dreaming. The pool was a perfect place to do that, but I also did it at school, and when I was fishing off Hornibrook Bridge. I daydreamed everywhere. Other times I'd be lying there on my towel and thinking about a girl and suddenly she would be standing over me, blocking the sun, and you'd have those visions where you think you are in love with her, and life couldn't be better than that.

In the world my brothers and I were living in, there was a lot of dark stuff going on in my house at that time. A lot of beautiful stuff as well, but our old man might be on a bender that could turn into quite a dangerous one when he got too firm a grasp of the bottle. But the next morning it was all good because you were hopping on your pushy and getting down to the Sandgate pool. When they put a footbridge over this busy four-lane highway that connected Bracken Ridge and Sandgate it meant we didn't have to risk our lives taking a shortcut across that crazy road. That footbridge enabled me to ride my pushbike past the Deagon Racecourse, through the Sandgate shops, down another little shortcut and then you'd be at the Sandgate swimming pool. That whole journey was magic because you were getting away; escaping to the pool where you'd spend 10 hours because you didn't want to go home.

On the way there, my best mate Ben Hart and I would

be thinking about girls and wondering who was going to be at the pool. Invariably there'd be a group of girls up there on the hill, and a group of girls under the shade of the trees, and a group of girls from St John Fisher, the local Catholic school, who were so far out of our league. They were unattainable so you had to proceed with caution. But deadset later you are in the water and you are just talking to a girl and she leans over and her body feels like the most amazing thing on earth and she plants a kiss on you, and you think, *Dammit I never want to leave this*. But invariably there'd be that sad moment when everyone says they have to go home and you don't want to go. We didn't want the dream of those days to end and we'd wait till the sun went down and we'd be kicked out of the Sandgate swimming pool.

Paul Kelly has this beautiful song called 'Deeper Water' and it's one of the greatest songs about coming of age. My coming of age happened at Sandgate swimming pool with me going into deeper water constantly. Learning to swim and progressing from the wading pool to the intermediate pool and then the big pool – deeper water. Getting into deeper water in my social life at the pool. Meeting girls – deeper water. Smoking cigarettes at the pool – deeper water. Wagging school and going to the pool and getting caught by a teacher who'd taken a class there – deeper water. Then even deeper water when my mates and I sneaked booze into the pool.

That pool was our paradise where we spent all day without sunscreen and got so sunburnt. It was right with me the whole way from age six until I left high school. When I was a little kid I'd run there as a place of pure freedom and wonder and towards the end I was going there as a 16-year-old working off hangovers. There's darkness and brutality in the Australian suburbs but there are also beautiful and magical places like the Sandgate swimming pool. It worked on all my senses – from the feel of the grass on that hill beneath my feet to the salty-fishy smell of that muddy Moreton Bay beachfront, the squawk of the seagulls, the smell of the popcorn and tomato sauce on a hot dog. That was all gold.

The ancient Greeks and Romans were always talking about the fountain as a source of life. Every Saturday and Sunday in summer I was making a pilgrimage to the fountain that was Sandgate pool. All my mates felt the pull of it and we'd scrounge around the house and sift through ashtrays for cash, and we'd ride along this endless beachfront right along Brighton and Sandgate and pool our money and get $2 worth of hot chips. Then we'd reach our destination, our Avalon, my Valhalla, the Sandgate swimming pool. I didn't go to church as a kid but that was my church – my sacred space – a pilgrimage to Sandgate swimming pool. That's where I was always going when I was a kid.

YUSRA METWALLY

Becoming an Auburn water baby

When Yusra Metwally was in primary school in the late 1990s and early 2000s, she loved gathering with the neighbourhood families at the Greenacre Swimming Centre, just around the corner from her family's south-west Sydney home. But in 2002 when she started wearing the hijab, swimming at public pools became problematic. After a lifeguard chastised her for wearing a non-lycra t-shirt, she no longer felt welcome at public pools.

My parents migrated from Egypt in the late 1980s and when I was born in 1990, we lived in Lakemba in south-west Sydney. Moves to Bankstown and Punch-bowl followed, and when I was about six we settled in nearby Greenacre, which is about 17 kilometres from central Sydney. That's when I started swimming at the Greenacre pool, which was just a few streets away from our house.

The Greenacre Swimming Centre had big, medium and little pools, but it was never a place for serious lap swimmers. It was classic suburbia where everyone in the neighbourhood congregated on hot days and had picnics on the huge areas of grass or under one of the gum trees near the back fence where you could see into the houses in the street behind. A high proportion of Arabic-speaking people lived in Greenacre, so there were lots of mothers in hijabs in the shade on the lawn or at the tables in the undercover area. My mother used to bring supplies of food and we'd come back to her every now and again and eat something, or get chips or an ice cream from the shop. I remember the place as very lively and inclusive and there was so much space for us kids to run around on the grass.

I loved the feeling of relief when we got in the water on those heatwave days that were always hotter in western Sydney than on the coast. When I was little, the wading pool, which was curved in shape, not rectangular like the deeper pools, was my favourite. My older brother and I, and later our two little sisters, would walk through the water, lie down on the white tiles and dip our heads under. Then we moved up to the medium-sized pool and finally the big pool, which I remember as 50 metres but was only 25 metres. In my primary-school years it seemed huge.

When I was six, I started swimming lessons at the pool and Mum has a photo of me being presented with a Learn to Swim certificate. I also took lessons with one of the schools I went to, an Islamic school on the corner of Greenacre Road and Banksia Avenue. It was just two streets away from the pool so we'd walk there in a line. I enjoyed those swimming lessons but I never quite got the breathing right. I'd have a go at swimming laps in the big pool and I'd think I was doing a really good job, flapping my arms over with my head out of the water.

My family also went to Sans Souci Beach and to the Birrong pool near Bankstown, which was much more of a swimming complex than the Greenacre pool. One time, when I was 10, I went to the Auburn Swimming Centre. That pool first opened in 1959, a time when Auburn was a much less multicultural place. Auburn is 24 kilometres west of the centre of Sydney and just over seven kilometres from Greenacre, and since the 1980s it has been a popular suburb for people from many nations, especially when they first arrived in Australia.

When I went to the Auburn Swimming Centre, I remember thinking it was much more colourful than the Greenacre pool. At Auburn, the tiles around the 50-metre pool and the smaller indoor pool were oblong shapes in shades of red, orange, pale pink, steel grey, black, mint green, light blue and white. There were blocks of colour everywhere – on the change room walls, on the seating and on the yellow grandstand by the Olympic-size pool. On the concrete area beside the pool were retro-style fixed umbrellas with seats in orange, blue and white.

The colourful design of the pool matched the lively atmosphere of the Sunday afternoon I spent there when it was only open to women. All of Mum's friends and all the women we knew in our community – young, old and in-between – were there. It was so nice to have the outdoor pool just for women, which meant that everyone could wear normal swimmers. I had on my favourite blue rash top with floral sleeves and matching lycra shorts, and most of the women wore one and two-pieces. It was an afternoon when everyone could let their hair down, literally. I remember watching the younger women take off their veils and noticing they dyed their hair, and seeing the older women's grey hair. I wasn't accustomed to seeing them often without their veils, so as a young girl I found it fascinating. It was a fun afternoon with all the different generations of women together – cooking a barbeque and sharing food, talking, laughing, swimming and relaxing in the water.

In my final years at primary school I continued swimming at the Greenacre pool, but once I started wearing the hijab in high school, swimming at pools became increasingly difficult for me. The burkini had been invented, but in my teenage years I thought it was ugly, and I refused to wear it. I struggled to find something I was comfortable wearing, and one time when I was at the pool at Olympic Park at Homebush, a lifeguard came up to me and said, 'You are not supposed to be wearing that.' The top I had on wasn't the correct lycra material. I had that feeling of being policed and not being welcome at public pools. When swimming carnivals came around each year at my state girls' high school, I didn't know what to wear, so I stayed home and studied and I thought I was great for getting ahead.

Pools were out of sight, out of mind during high school, and when I was studying law at university and for the first few years I was working. Then in August 2016, just before the Rio Olympics, I heard of a Syrian swimmer with the same first name as me who was a member of the Refugee Olympic Team. Yusra Mardini's heroic story sparked something in me, hearing how she jumped into cold water to lighten the load on an overcrowded boat of asylum seekers, then pushed the boat towards the Greek shore for several hours, and I started thinking about swimming and pools again.

Around this time at my work we were talking about wellbeing and dabbling in ideas for lunchtime activities and my director asked if anyone wanted to join him for a swim at North Sydney Pool. Initially I thought, *Really, at lunch?* But I decided to try it out and took the plunge and bought a burkini. Fortunately, there were a lot more fashionable styles by then and even the iconic brand Speedo was making one, which normalised it as a form of swimwear. So, after a number of years of not going to pools, one sunny lunchtime I joined my director and a few of our colleagues in my new burkini at the magnificent North Sydney Olympic Pool.

It's so grand swimming there underneath the arch of the Sydney Harbour Bridge, and when I got in the salt water it was like being born again. I felt that moment of initial release, like on hot days back at the Greenacre pool, and being hugged by the coolness of the water. I felt so free, and it was wonderful having that time to relax and disconnect from work. I kept saying, 'Wow,' to myself and thinking, *This is what I have been missing out on*. I watched people swimming laps and I tried to have a go but I was pretty much drowning. I realised I needed to go back to basics and learn to swim again.

I couldn't return to lessons at my childhood pool at Greenacre because the council closed it down in 2016. It was such a shame because that pool was very central to the small community there and provided respite on those heatwave western Sydney days. It's remained locked up since then and the only signs of life are hundreds of ibises that have taken residence at the pool. There's a sign on the gate saying:

> *This facility will remain closed until further notice due to structural issues with the pools. Alternate facilities are available less than five kilometres away at Birrong and Roselands.*

So instead I went to the Roselands pool, where they had adult lessons just for women on Sunday mornings. I did two lots of those lessons and when I finished I got a certificate, just like when I was six at the Greenacre pool. I realised I needed to keep practising regularly and so I decided to start a swimming group called Swim Sisters to inspire women from all backgrounds, walks of life, fitness levels, shapes and sizes to go for a swim. I organised and took part in weekly stroke correction classes run by my friend Fadila Chafic, and I finally mastered breathing and freestyle. Since then my swimming has improved and I have re-connected with the Auburn pool where I had that wonderful experience of swimming with a community of women when I was 10.

It's called the Ruth Everuss Aquatic Centre now after another inspiring woman, who at 16 was a silver medallist in a relay event at the 1960 Rome Olympics, and later taught swimming, including classes just for women, and trained squads at the Auburn Swimming Centre. In 2017 the Centre was totally redeveloped, so it's not quite as colourful as it was in 2000, but it has become a very welcoming place for Muslim women, with part of the renovation involving installing curtains in the indoor pool so that several nights a week women can have privacy when they swim. As well, every Sunday afternoon there are women-only swimming sessions and water safety classes. I have a season pass to the pool and each Wednesday night I join a group of women, many Muslim but some not, who take part in stroke correction and swimming lessons with my Swim Sisters group. On Wednesday nights we don't have the whole pool like that day when I was 10, but we do have a lane and the same feeling of camaraderie as we all come together at the pool. Since giving birth to my son in March 2019, I'm also at the pool for his Splish Splash babies' water familiarisation class.

I've even returned to swimming at Olympic Park, where I was told more than 10 years ago that my swimwear wasn't acceptable. Since 2017, I've been taking part in the MS 24-hour Mega Swim there, which is great fun, like being at a slumber party with all your friends. The second and third years I did it, it was Ramadan, but we managed because not everyone in our Swim Sisters team was Muslim. Some girls also felt comfortable to swim while they were fasting and I did the night shift just before it was time to stop eating at 4 a.m.

Now I always have my swimmers, goggles and towel in my car so that wherever I am I can go for a swim. I always experience a special joy being immersed in the water at McIver's Ladies Baths at Coogee, Australia's last surviving women-only pool, where I had a relaxing swim before I went into labour with my first child. I am a strong believer in having some women-only spaces and it's wonderful to go to McIver's where there's less testosterone and a calmer, non-competitive atmosphere.

When I turn up at pools in my black burkini in areas of Sydney where there aren't many Muslim people, occasionally I get a few looks because they are not used to seeing Muslim women swimming. But I don't pay attention to what others think any more and I don't believe I am doing anything extraordinary. Just like everybody else, I am there to swim and most of the time people are very welcoming. I've come full circle from those carefree early childhood days at Greenacre pool and I'm an Aussie water baby again. Now I just have to do something about reopening the Greenacre pool.

BRYAN BROWN

Bumping into life
at Bankstown Baths

When Bryan Brown was growing up in Panania in
south-west Sydney in the 1950s and early 1960s,
there were three hubs of social life outside of school:
the picture theatre, the church and the municipal
baths. The baths at nearby Bankstown had one of
Sydney's first Olympic-size chlorine pools when they
opened in 1933. Twenty-five years later, when young
Bryan was living in the area, the pool was still going
strong, and from the ages of 11 to 15, that was
where he wanted to be.

Back in the 1950s and early 1960s, lots of young families moved to the Bankstown area for the War Service homes and the Housing Commission homes around Panania, Revesby and East Hills. My mother Molly and younger sister Kristine and I lived in a Housing Commission home in Panania and, like all the other residents, we went to the pool at Bankstown as it was the only one in the area. It was a place of enormous life and where you wanted to be on the weekend. It was hot out there in summer and you couldn't wait to dive into the pool.

I first went there when I was about 11, with my mother and my sister, to have swimming lessons. We lived near the Georges River at Panania and I suppose if you lived near a river you'd eventually learn to swim. But Mum wanted us to learn properly, so she booked us in for swimming lessons at the baths. Learning to swim was an incredibly important part of being an Australian kid and Bankstown Baths was a fantastic place to learn that essential life skill. After our series of lessons my sister and I got certificates saying we could swim 25 yards, and that was the beginning of swimming for us.

Right from the start I loved swimming. I loved being in the water, mucking around and diving down deep, and I loved the feel of the water over my body. And once I could swim, I could get the bus to the baths instead of going with Mum. Learning to swim was the start of becoming more independent and moving from being a little boy to being a big boy. The bus trip from Panania to Bankstown was seven miles and most weekends in summer I took that ride down the bottom of the hill with blokes who lived in my street.

One of the greatest things about the Bankstown Baths was the smell of chlorine. I used to walk into those baths and go down into the boys' dressing rooms and you'd walk through water, a little sort of pond that cleaned your feet, before you could go out into the swimming pool. As you started to ascend the steps to go to the pool there was an overwhelming smell of chlorine and you knew you were at the Bankstown Baths. It's nothing like the smell of chlorine now.

The pool was pretty standard. There was a smaller children's pool and a 55-yard pool which had a high diving board and a small one. The boards were part of the 55-yard pool and under the diving tower it was 10 feet deep. My mates and I tended to hang around the middle of that pool. We did a lot of running and jumping and bombing each other. We splashed around and chased each other and wrestled in the water. It was all pretty unstructured.

Sometimes you'd get bumped by a bigger kid and he might try and hold your head under water for a while. In that moment it didn't feel too bloody good because for a second or two you thought you're going to drown. And then he lets you up and you splutter and gasp for breath. But you also come up having understood a bit more about what life was all about. I suppose these days you'd call that boy a bully, and some of the other bigger boys who bumped you around a bit. But I just called them smart-arses. You learned not to get caught around that sort of bloke again and you learned how to handle things. If someone jumped in or bombed and hit you on the shoul-der – well, you learned to get out of their road. It was all just part of growing up.

The other great thing about that period was Bank-stown Baths had John and Ilsa Konrads training there with Don Talbot as their coach. And you sat there in awe of these great swimmers, two young immigrant kids from Latvia who had won Olympic medals. That was pretty exciting. We'd sit on the side of the pool watching them. We knew exactly who they were. They were world record holders and Olympic champions and they were at our pool. They were training in one lane while we all jumped in and out and splashed each other in the next lane. And Don Talbot was a big presence there as well. You didn't get any bigger than Don Talbot and he was the coach of those two.

There was an area at the back of Bankstown Baths where there was a lot of bush and that's where the bodgies and widgies used to go. We'd be running around in our Speedos but down the back were these blokes and girls in their jeans and leather jackets. They'd be kissing and cuddling and you'd try and have a little sneak and look around the bushes, but you weren't game to go in too far. One of those blokes would probably hammer you. It was a pretty exotic, colourful old place the Bankstown Baths.

It was a place of enormous life. A fantastic place for all the young people between the ages of eight up to 30 – and if you were 30 you probably looked really old to us. Those baths initiated me not just to swimming but a whole other understanding of life – who were the right people to hang around with and who were not. It was a place where you worked things out yourself and learned about friendship and loyalty.

Mostly I think of the Bankstown Baths as an exciting place. I went every Sunday and looked forward to it. I couldn't wait. After being around for more than 50 years, in 1984 the baths were closed. I didn't really hear about that until one night in 2013 when I was invited to a poetry slam at the Bankstown Arts Centre. On that same night they were celebrating the eightieth birthday of the pool and I was knocked out when I realised that the Bankstown Baths were now an arts centre. I was happy because it was still a hub, but in a much bigger way because it was a hub for young people, middle-aged and older people as well. If the baths had been filled in and there were flats on them it wouldn't have made me happy. But as an arts centre, the place was still fulfilling a community function – very different to when I was growing up, but just as important.

I sat there in that audience of Lebanese, Egyptian, Chinese, Pakistani, Indian and Anglo Australians and I remembered how important this building was to me 50 years before. And later when I became a patron of the Bankstown Arts Centre I got to meet my hero John Konrads again. He was also a patron and when I met him, I was able to say: 'Mate, I used to sit on the edge of the baths here and I used to idolise you.' It was great to meet John and for both of us to be at the place where the Bankstown Baths used to be and to see that it's still playing a cultural role in the local community and, just like the baths were, it's a vibrant place full of life.

TESS LEA

Daydreaming underwater at the Parap Pool

When Tess Lea was born in 1966, they were still culling saltwater crocodiles in the Timor Sea surrounding Darwin. While Tess and her family did occasionally wade into the sea, it was never a safe option for cooling off in Darwin's tropical climate. Alternatives were friends' backyard pools or plunging into the fresh water at Berry Springs on the outskirts of town. For Tess, the answer was the Parap Pool, across the road from where she lived for the first eight years of her life.

Parap Pool was the grand dame of the four public pools in Darwin, as it was the first one to be built. It opened in 1960, six years before I was born, and was perhaps two lap lengths from our house. Back then Parap was a working-class suburb where lots of Indigenous, migrant and Housing Commission families lived. The pool was the meeting space for the people who lived in the suburb, but most of them weren't doing swimming training there like me. They were there to cool off on those hot, humid Darwin days in a time when there was no such thing as air conditioning.

When I was a toddler I was already an official member of the Darwin Swimming Club based at Parap Pool – apparently ABC TV did a story on me as the youngest club member. Mum tells me I could swim before I could walk. I imagine I was learning to swim in utero because swimming meant so much to her and still does. She introduced all her four children to swimming when we were very young and joined us up to the club.

Parap Pool was built to yard length, not metres, so once metric-length pools came in it wasn't Olympic-standard. There was a square-shaped toddlers' pool that was only a foot or so deep, and a big 55-yard pool with a deep end that seemed cavernous to me as a small child. And there were two diving boards – a one-metre and one that was about three metres off the ground, a tower to a little girl's eyes.

It was a big deal to be allowed to dive off the high diving board, but eventually it was removed because it interfered with the starting blocks. It was also a big deal to go down to the bottom and pop your ears and come back up and take another deep breath and go back down again. Beyond the shallow end of the pool was a small play-ground area with those old-style metal maypoles with the chains that knocked kids out, hard wooden swings, and a quite hot, precarious and sharp-edged metal slippery dip.

There wasn't much vegetation around the pool in those early days, but there were some grand old rubber trees, a rare thing for Darwin – our trees usually got pushed over by cyclones or termites. There were lots of green-ant nests in those rubber trees and ginger ants combing the grass, so you didn't put your towel down and sunbake because you'd be bitten alive within five seconds. As locals we knew the grey dust mounds heralded the ginger ants, but visitors didn't and a few minutes after they'd sat down they'd be attacked by swarms of these tiny, vicious ants.

I spent hours and hours in the Parap Pool. If I wasn't training with the club I was holding my breath sitting on the bottom at the shallow end. I'd take a deep breath, push myself under, and then slowly let all my air out as I sat straight-legged on the bottom and played imaginary games. I'd make up stories and listen to my bubble sounds and observe the bodies swim past. I could hold my breath for quite a while and then eventually I'd come back up for air. The locals knew I did this as I was there every day, so they weren't alarmed by a young girl sitting on the bottom of the pool. But non-regulars didn't and I was pulled out of my reveries a couple of times by adults who thought I needed to be rescued. And then they'd tell me off when they discovered I was just playing!

I also enjoyed holding onto my ankles and making a circle backwards with my body. I was very flexible and so I'd circle and circle and every time I came to the surface I would grab air and go around again. I kept doing it for ages and ages – lost in my own little world. I was quite happy on my own at the pool but I was never really on my own because there was always a bunch of older kids there who knew me and adults keeping an eye on us all.

We had a succession of pool managers and occasionally there were some sensible ones. 'Do not run on the concrete, Teresa,' they'd call out on the PA. If old man Jeffs found you running on the concrete he'd make you scrub the goddamn tiles on the big pool. The 55-yard pool had a funny guttering system. The edge sloped inward, meeting a gutter with this curved black tile you could hold onto at the side of the pool, but when you tumble-turned you could smash your ankle on it. Water didn't always flow into the gutter and so mucky stuff could gather in the corner and an oily residue would get on the pale sky-blue tiles with their black lip. We were constantly being conscripted to scrub those tiles with a toothbrush, which was the worst job ever – like prison duty.

Because the Northern Territory wasn't and still isn't a state, and maybe because we had such a small population, we didn't swim in state or national swimming contests, but we could represent Darwin in country competitions. As a result, I went to all these pools in regional towns in the Northern Territory, South Australia and Queensland: Tennant Creek, Whyalla, Bordertown and Gympie. We'd end up at these strange little country hotels and swim in the town pools, which were often only 25 metres or the old-style 33-yard pools.

The one I remember most was in Tennant Creek

where I was billeted with a family and had to eat this horrible thick fake cheese and drink powdered milk; there were so many flies we wore nets over our heads the whole time. Those flies were sticky and thick and they'd be crawling all over you and in your mouth. When we had to go in a swimming race, we'd keep our fly nets on till just before the gun went off and then we'd whip them off our heads and dive into the pool.

In the dry season locals wouldn't use Parap Pool as much because for them it would be too cold. It still gets over 30 degrees in the dry season but for Darwin people it is so much cooler than the searing heat and high humidity in the wet season. After early morning training in the dry season we would be shivering and we'd need our tracksuits. If we spent a lot of time in the water on those dry season days, we'd cool down really quickly when we got out, so we'd often bring something warm to the pool to rug up.

In the wet season we were never cold, and we kept asking for shade cloths to be put over the pool as it was too blazingly hot. Eventually they did, but the first ones were simply triangles which hung low over the water in places. They were a temptation for kids to jump on and slide off, so very quickly they were wrecked. During what we called 'the build-up', before the monsoon really hit, everything in Darwin, including the pool, would get tepid and the chlorine would get a whole lot stronger. I used to wonder why they put so much more chlorine in but now I understand it was because they were in a constant battle trying to fight evaporation. Contrary to what you would think, there's as much if not more evaporation in a moisture-saturated environment as a dry one.

Before Cyclone Tracy came in 1974, I used to pile mangoes into a wheelbarrow and set up at the entrance to the pool and sell the Bowens for 10 cents and the Stringies for 5 cents. We had a Bowen mango tree in our yard so I'd get the Bowens from there and the Stringies I collected around the racecourse. Stringies were a smaller mango, longer and skinnier, and as the name suggests they were stringier with heaps more stuff to get stuck in your teeth. I charged more for the Bowens because a good mango is always a Bowen. People who came to the pool bought them and I'd usually go home with an empty wheelbarrow and a pocket full of coins or I'd treat myself to an ice cream at the pool shop.

The afternoon before Cyclone Tracy arrived I was training in the pool with the Darwin Swimming Club as if everything was normal. There'd been multiple cyclones before this one and there was fatigue with preparing for them when so many had been fizzers – and it was Christmas Eve. I remember stopping training for a few minutes to listen to the manager's announcement over the PA about a cyclone coming tonight. He was having some kind of Christmas party and he got onto the microphone and spoke in a very sloshed and slurred voice. After that we kept on with our training. That night the roof blew off our house and a bit of wall smashed into my finger as I lay in bed. I spent the rest of the night bunkered down in our kitchen with my family and some neighbours; I sat on my brother's knee with the cat on my lap as the adults passed around a bottle of Tia Maria.

The next day everything was flattened. You could see about 20 kilometres across Darwin and Parap Pool was filled with car bodies and palm trees. It was a complete dump site. There were a couple of backyard pools in our street so we used one of them to get water, which we boiled on our gas stove – we were the only family for miles around who had a gas stove instead of electricity. A few days afterwards, my mother, my sisters and I were evacuated to Brisbane. Dad and my brother, who was 10 years older than me, stayed behind to help in the clean-up.

In Brisbane I went to a school in a northern suburb called Humpybong, just south of Redcliffe, and I remember mourning for my multicultural Darwin school. At my Brisbane school there were no Aboriginal kids, no Greek kids, Chinese kids or Vietnamese kids – all the kids I'd grown up with – and I remember noticing it as an eight-year-old.

When we came back to Darwin about six months later, Dad, being a surveyor, had worked out that if Tracy had hit at high tide, suburbs like Parap would have been completely flooded. So he took us further away from the sea breezes to an area called Ludmilla, which, from a surveyor's point of view, was much safer as it was on slightly higher ground. We are just talking rises in Darwin, so we weren't on top of a hill. We no longer lived across the road from Parap Pool, so I couldn't just toddle over and have a swim. It was a hot journey on foot to get there, so I would cycle over or be picked up by another family. But the spontaneity of it was gone and my relationship with the pool became focused on training.

After the cyclone, the pool remained pretty much the same except they got rid of the rank and dank change rooms and built new ones and a club room where we could keep all our equipment. The rubber trees miraculously survived, as did the scrubby row of crotons near the back fence – a favourite spot when I was a kid. We were like little rabbits ducking in and out of that scrub bordering the fence-line. It was free of ginger ants and we'd play hidey and marbles there. When the club had fundraising nights at the pool, or a time trial followed by a barbeque, all of us kids would sneak off into those spaces when the parents weren't paying attention and get up to all sorts of things like spin the bottle or truth or dare or telling terrible stories to scare each other.

When I was about 11, a new elite squad was created from the best swimmers at Darwin's three public pools – Parap, Nightcliff and Casuarina – and we were bussed over to train in a pool at the army barracks. A man called Captain Bloomfield, who was an ex-swimmer, trained us. He was much more systematic about training and our times went through the roof. He obviously had a fair bit of knowledge but training was no longer a family-run affair. I missed the camaraderie of the Darwin Swimming Club at Parap Pool and all those families that I'd grown up with. It wasn't fun any more.

At the same time, I was hitting teenage-hood and I wasn't sure if being a serious swimmer was my identity any more. Between 12 and 17, I only went to Parap Pool if my friends were going there to splash around and gossip. I became really low-key about being a swimmer and I didn't put my hand up for swimming carnivals. I thought I was too cool for the pool. There was quite a lot going on at home – problems between my parents and with Dad's business – so instead of swimming I took up smoking and all sorts of unhealthy habits like hanging around with the wrong kids at the wrong end of town in the dead of night.

I went through that whole period of being a complete rebel. In the latter part of those rebellious years I broke into the Parap Pool one night with a group of four or maybe six friends and we pushed each other in the water. I think we broke a lock or we might have climbed over a fence. Another kid who lived in the street had noticed odd movements and shadows in the pool so he called the police and we got busted. Even though he would not have been able to tell who was there, in that completely illogical way teenage brains work, we were outraged that someone we knew had dobbed us in. The coppers decided to let us off, but they told us not to do it again in very stern terms, and if we did there would be trouble. It was enough. My career as a rebel was pretty low-grade.

Eventually I realised that I needed to get my act together and so I returned to study in my final two years of school and after that spent six months travelling through

Canada and America with a friend. When I came back I was actually quite depressed, as my parents had split up and my father's business had gone bankrupt. I had also piled on weight in North America, so I went back to Parap Pool and did my own little program every day. By now it was 1984 and the pool had a very sensible manager. The facilities were well looked after, with no cigarette butts on the side of the pool or band-aids or sticking plaster in the water. It was beautifully kept but it was also threatened with closure, so with Mum and others I got involved in a campaign to save the pool.

The government wanted to close it down because as well as Nightcliff and Casuarina there was a new pool out at Palmerston, a satellite city. The government's thinking was that we didn't need Parap Pool any more because it was old and leaking and it wasn't even Olympic stand-ard. It was also on valuable real estate and they wanted to turn it into a townhouse complex. We got everyone to sign a petition and made placards and protested outside the pool. A whole lot of the old families got involved and proved that there was a desire for the pool beyond people just training there and we saved it from closing.

Before I left Darwin in 1985 to go to university in Perth, a few of the city's heavy-duty storms came in, so a couple of times I was able to swim through those storms at Parap Pool. It had been one of my most favourite things to do at the pool as a child, and it was wonderful to experience it again before I left there for university. If there were lightning storms the manager would chuck everyone out of the water, but if it was just one of Darwin's heavy-duty storms you were still allowed to swim.

It was the most magical thing to do and was one of those rare occasions in Darwin when the air would be cooler than the water. The power and thickness of the raindrops in those storms was incredible and as I swam I could see these streaks of water spearing like diamonds over and over. These diamond threads were pearling and pearling all around me and making this a four-dimensional sensory experience. Parts of my arms were being hammered by the water and the rain pelting down hard drowned out all the familiar, comforting pool sounds. But when I put my head in the water I could still hear my breathing and bubble-making and see the wash around me.

It was otherworldly swimming in those storms – the water in the pool assumed new qualities and the light became much darker. Instead of the usual bright blues on a sunny day, the colours were much deeper navies, purples and dark greys as multiple diamond spheres appeared and disappeared around me. Usually I was on my own because few others swam in those storms. They were mesmerising – all thought was suspended and I was completely captivated by the splendour of the experience.

For the past eight or so years I haven't lived in Darwin, but I still love to return to visit family and friends, and in Christmas 2018 I went back to the Parap Pool. Fortunately, it had survived myriad threats of closure and hadn't been turned into a townhouse complex. Between 2016 and 2017 it was totally redeveloped and now it's not a couple of centimetres too long, there's no funny guttering system and no drunk pool managers. Today it's a beautiful pool with a lot more shading and, on the day I swam there, it had a wonderful atmosphere with a cross-section of people ranging from young families with babies to teenagers and older people enjoying the new facilities.

At the entrance there's an extraordinary art piece called *Under the Surface* depicting the interplay of water, light and movement, which was definitely one of the ways I experienced the pool as a child. Another addition is a memory wall honouring the history of the pool, and as I swam up and down, all sorts of memories came back to me – how Parap Pool was my place, especially in those years before Cyclone Tracy. I had visions of my mother passing on her love of swimming to me and how, apart from a break in my teenage years, I have always been a water girl.

As I swam, I thought about what I would record if I could post a memory on that wall, and in the end, I settled on one of those days when I was in a butterfly race for the Darwin Swimming Club. I pictured myself executing my favourite stroke and as I did I got lost in the feeling of being completely immersed in the rhythm of butterfly. Ah, to be that fit again, able to pace Parap Pool as the stone that skims across the top of the water!

Bay pools

MICK THOMAS

Everyone was welcome in Geelong

When Mick Thomas was a child in the 1960s and 70s, his father's job as an electrical engineer for the State Electricity Commission (SES) took them to several Victorian country towns – Yallourn, Gippsland, Colac and Horsham. In each place Mick and his family connected with the local pool, the focal point of those hot inland towns in summer. In 1969, when Mick was nine, the family moved to Geelong, less than 80 kilometres from Melbourne on the south-western side of Port Phillip Bay. In Geelong, Mick discovered the Eastern Beach Swimming Enclosure, expansive saltwater baths built on Corio Bay in the late 1930s.

When we moved to Geelong I was getting to that age where I was awkward about meeting people. As a new kid in town, I remember thinking it was really important for me to go to the Eastern Beach Swimming

Enclosure and hook up with the friends I was making at school. The first time I went there with the kid who lived next door to us, I remember him saying, 'Look at this.' He grabbed a mussel clinging to a pylon under the timber decking, opened it up and ate it. It was a very different experience to swimming in chlorine at the pool in Horsham, although one time we did have to become deep-sea divers to find my uncle's dentures.

You could get to the Eastern Beach Swimming Enclosure along the foreshore or from Eastern Beach Road, high above Corio Bay, where there was a white Spanish-style staircase that led down to the baths. It was commanding, that staircase, and halfway down there was a fountain with statues of cranes and tortoises. From that point you got a great view over the swimming enclosure. Closer to the shore was a round concrete wading pool filled with chlorinated water and a fountain. Beyond that was the arc-shaped tidal pool that enclosed nearly three and a half hectares of salt water that flowed in and out with the tide from Corio Bay. Curving around the water was a massive timber deck and within the enclosure were diving boards, a diving tower, a floating island, slides, and anchor buoys we called sailors' hats. They were about five metres in diameter, big enough for about 20 kids to cram on and rock violently.

In the late 1960s and 1970s, Geelong was a big industrial centre. It was home to the Ford Motor Company at Norlane in the north, the Shell refinery, the Alcoa aluminium smelter, the cement works, and International

Harvesters, a company that made tractors, trucks and other agricultural equipment. These industries attracted migrants to Geelong – including Italians, Greeks and people from the former Yugoslavia – and each wave of migrants adopted the Eastern Beach Swimming Enclosure. It was the communal place, the social hub of the town, especially as there wasn't much else to do in Geelong at that time. The city centre was just a place for office workers, so when people wanted to meet up or go out, they went to the foreshore, and specifically Eastern Beach.

In summer all the different groups had their tea there on Friday nights on the grassy slopes above the baths. Our tea was just sandwiches, nothing as exotic or tasty as what the Greek, Italian or Croatian families were eating. We lived in Hamlyn Heights in the western part of Geelong, and I remember on those Friday nights Mum and Dad would spot families we knew on the lawn. On Christmas Day, all the Greek and Italian families gathered there.

In that first year in Geelong I had swimming lessons at the local Olympic pool at Norlane, where our school carnivals were held, but in the holidays we tended to go to the Eastern Beach Swimming Enclosure. On weekends I went there with my mate Ian, and by the time we were 11 or 12 we were riding our bikes down there. Within the baths was this enormous buoy-type structure with big steel pegs coming out the sides so kids could climb right up the top of it. It would take 15 kids to drag it sideways into the water and when one kid was right up on top, everyone would let go and that kid would fly through the air for 15 metres. If it went wrong, the thing would smack someone in the mouth. It was incredibly dangerous and there must have been kids who lost teeth. I also remember walking out to the end of a pier and playing on one of the treadmill wheels. You'd lie flat on your face and spin over and over, but if you didn't let go at the right time you'd smash your head. In the middle there was a huge island platform 40 feet square with more treadmill wheels and slides, which everyone kept piling onto until there would be 50 or 60 kids rocking it.

My father occasionally swam at Eastern Beach, but most of the time he went to Rippleside, which was nearly three kilometres north along the foreshore. In much earlier days the Rippleside Swimming Club had held races and lessons there, but by the 1970s there were just two bits of floating timber between two piers that marked out 50 metres. My dad was big on going there at 6 a.m., even in the colder months. He wasn't military in any way but he had that ascetic attitude of someone who'd lived through the Depression and World War II. He believed cold water was good for you and he'd get me to come with him.

On those grey mornings, he'd dive straight in. I'd stand shivering on the pier, saying, 'Do I have to?' Eventually I'd get in and the water was so cold it took my breath away. I never wanted to go in but now Dad's long gone, it's a memory of a time when I felt close to him. A couple of years ago I wrote a song about swimming with him at Rippleside with the morning frost on our pink skin and Dad laughing as he dived in.

As I got older it became a rite of passage to meet girls at the pool at Eastern Beach and afterwards we'd get a milkshake a bit further along the foreshore from a lady who had this ornate booth where she made her own syrups for milkshakes. It was a real iconic place back in my teenage years. Around this time there was talk in our house about another move. In the State Electricity Commission, the only way to get a promotion was to apply for one in a different town. Dad wanted to be a branch manager and was looking around at places where a position was coming up. But repeated protests from my older brother and my sister and me about not wanting to move again meant we stayed put in Geelong.

In those later teenage years I took up surfing at the beaches near Geelong and swam less at the baths at Eastern Beach. In 1979, when I moved to Melbourne to do an Arts degree, I left surfing behind and ultimately my life became all about music. Mum and Dad stayed in Geelong and I remember during the 1980s and 90s it went through some hard times with the closure of a number of industries. When the Pyramid Building Society, founded in Geelong in the late 1950s, collapsed in 1990, it had a bad effect on Geelong's economy. It seemed to coincide with the diving tower at the Eastern Beach Swimming Enclosure sliding into the sea.

Fortunately, the town banded together and the Eastern Beach Restoration Appeal was formed to raise funds to restore the place. The appeal secured some government funding, and more than 4000 people contributed by joining in the 'buy a plank' campaign, which enabled them to have their name on a brass plate on the new promenade. The restoration of the promenade, diving tower and slide island was based on the original 1938 plans, and just before Christmas in 1993, it reopened in all its former glory.

When I reflect back on my time at the Eastern Beach Swimming Enclosure from the age of nine till my late teens, it links up with all the pools I've swum in throughout my life. In 1984, when I formed my band Weddings Parties Anything, a guy in the music world said to me, 'If you're going to do this for a living, you've got to keep healthy and keep some sort of physical activity in your life.' So I returned to the pool. I've never been a champion swimmer but I enjoy doing laps and I like how pools are pretty democratic places where there's a real mixture of status groups and ages.

In those country towns I lived in as a young child, the pool was crucial to the life of the place and somewhere to take cousins and friends when they came to visit. In Geelong, the Eastern Beach Swimming Enclosure was the congregating place where each generation of migrants – the Italians, the Greeks, the Serbs and Croatians – were welcomed. This continues today, and when I swam there recently, there were lots of African families gathered at the pool.

TONY DOHERTY

Captured in cool green wonder

Tony Doherty grew up close to the Lane Cove River in the Sydney suburb now known as Riverview. From the late 1930s till the early 1950s that river and a small inlet known as Tambourine Bay were his world of boyhood adventure, their waters and mysterious muddy mangroves teeming with life. The baths at Tambourine Bay, part of the property of his school, St Ignatius College Riverview, were where he learned to swim.

Often on a steamy Sunday morning my father, my older brother and I would set off down the road for the baths on Tambourine Bay. The area took its name from the colourful legend of a former convict woman, 'Tambourine Nell', who was believed to have played her musical instrument on a distant hill. Complete with towels and sandals we'd walk about a kilometre down the road before navigating along a scrubby bush track, stepping carefully between large eucalypts, overgrown lantana and black-berry bushes. The thrum of the cicadas was deafening as we walked single file along that not-well-beaten path, home to various species of lizards, the occasional goanna, the rustle of snakes and 'tick bushes', the abode of little brutes that would often have to be dug out of our scalps. This was the world of a future Indiana Jones.

One of the fascinating features of this trek was a murky water-filled hole known locally as the Convict Pool. It was roughly cut into the sandstone and was about six metres square. The water was fetid and slime-covered, almost hidden by vines and bush, but it was unmistakably a pool. We never failed to give it our attention and wonder at its origin. In his rough jocular fashion my father would threaten to throw me in if I wasn't an obedient son. It was a place from some forgotten time, with a tinge of danger about it. Snakes would be found near the water. A com-pelling mixture designed to fire the imagination.

After paying our respects to the Convict Pool we would continue along the track, scrambling over slippery sandstone rocks – quite a feat for a little tacker of four or five. By this stage I'd usually be on my father's back. Finally, at journey's end, we'd break through the bush and arrive at a wooden-fenced pool sparkling in the sun on the western side of Tambourine Bay.

The sight of it was pure joy. The pool was rectangu-lar in shape, a little more than 30 metres long, equipped with a diving board at each end, ladders dropping into the water (almost superfluous when the tide was high), and solid timber-planked decks. It even had rough change rooms hewn out of rock. In my memory, the southern end of the deck is always bathed in bright early morning sunshine. Often a few aged Jesuit priests would be taking in the sun, oblivious of later warnings about the danger of melanoma. Life was simpler then. Our hosts from River-view College who had built these private baths never hesitated to offer hospitality to any locals who found some time to splash there as well.

My brother and I would race each other to get out of our clothes and into the water. The contest was grossly unfair. Peter was six years older than me and I couldn't yet swim. Dancing with impatience, I had to wait for my dad to inflate a rubber swimming ring and secure it carefully with a stopper. The big brother always beat me to the water.

One momentous day, when I was five or six, I left the rubber ring on the wooden deck and jumped in. Thrashing around in the water, flailing arms and legs with a mouth half-full of Lane Cove River, I felt the strong arm of my brother reach out and save me. Somehow, I managed a primitive dog paddle. It was hilarious for all the spectators but not for me. To this day, it is a vivid moment in my early memories. There is one great question I ponder to this day: how do we swim? One moment you sink like a stone, the next you discover the magic of buoyancy. How does that happen? Learning to relax, I suppose. Learning to trust yourself. Learning to trust the water, which holds so much of our ancestral past. Appreciating the wisdom of play, perhaps. Whatever is the magic of it, learning to trust the water and swim may be one of the significant rites of passage for us all, carrying much wisdom into the many experiences of our life. Letting go of the shallow end of the pool, letting go of the rubber rings of life, are momentous instances in our search for freedom and being our own person.

From that day my dog paddle improved and my love of salty water deepened, especially at high tide. At Christmas, we would enjoy the wonder of king tides, when the baths were a peerless place to swim. They carry delicious memories of diving into a world of cool green wonder.

After a couple of exhausting hours, the three of us would make the trek home through the overgrown bush, back up to a road so hot that the heat would scorch through the soles of our sandals. We'd walk in the door sunburnt, hungry and happy to the aroma of a classic Sunday baked dinner and my mother inspecting the potatoes roasting in the oven. She never joined us for the swim. I'm not even sure whether she ever learned to swim. Now that's an embarrassing admission.

What was never in doubt was her ability to produce a mouth-watering meal for a ravenous family. Nor was her ambition for the future of her two sons and her daughter. It was because of our single-minded mother, her persuasive manner and charm, that Peter and I ended up going to St Ignatius College Riverview, less than a mile away down the hill. Dad was a draftsman on the railways and our family had few financial resources, but my mother negotiated a bursary that almost amounted to free tuition for both of us. The exceptional generosity of the Jesuits, not only in sharing their pool but sharing their school, was never forgotten.

The Tambourine Bay swimming pool continued to shape my life and, on one special occasion when I was seven, soon after I'd started at Riverview in 1942, my sense of morality and honesty. The school had a rule that students must keep within certain boundaries on the playground. A sensible restriction in such a wild, bushy environment. It was impressed on us that to move beyond these limits was a serious infraction of the rule 'Never go out of bounds!' On normal school days, the swimming pool on Tambourine Bay was definitely regarded as out of bounds unless we were accompanied by a teacher. However, the drive of little boys on an impossibly hot summer's day overcame all sense of reason.

I and my eight-year-old partner in crime decided that in this record heat a swim at lunchtime was the only thing that would save our young lives, so we decided to make a break for it. Down we went through the bush and swam to our hearts' content. Alas, this was an era when children didn't even have a watch (much less a smart phone) and to our horror we lost track of time and were late back for the first period after lunch – significantly, a religion class. We announced ourselves and slipped into our seats, hair tousled and still dripping, this time with a nervous sweat.

The teacher was a Jesuit called Patrick Sullivan, a gentle soul and a luminously good man, who called on us to explain ourselves. We stood before the dock, scarcely able to do anything else but tell the whole story. Expulsion from school? Perhaps. Held in disgrace before all of our contemporaries? Likely. Facing punishment of one kind or another for the rest of the term? Almost certainly. Our gentle judge and executioner stood before us looking stern. His words are etched among my most formative memories. 'For telling the truth, we will just forget about it. Sit down and open your books.' It's hard to estimate how such childhood experiences shape young lives. The lessons of transparent honesty, I imagine, have regrettably been broken in later years, but the ability to judge others' actions with sympathy and understanding may be traced back to that day I so flagrantly broke the College rule by visiting that pool.

Other times I went to the baths officially with the school, and even though I didn't have any lessons, eventually I learned to swim a length overarm, another moment of achievement. We always had a lot of fun jumping in and out of the water, leaping off the wooden diving boards and playing a game called the greasy pole. It involved two competitors sliding onto separate poles that stretched out over the water at the deep end, locking their legs around the pole, holding one arm behind their back and then with their weapon, a pillow, attempting to knock their opponent off the other pole and into the water. It was terrific fun.

Those baths on the Lane Cove River were where I first experienced the absolute joy of immersion. Looking back over the eight decades of my life, I am coming to realise that swimming and my love of water continue to knit together many of the 'shaping' moments in my life. Today, still, I try to swim each morning in Sydney Harbour and I hold those sunny memories of Tambourine Bay and its wooden baths close to my heart. Someone once suggested to me that an extraordinary percentage of living matter on the planet exists beneath the water: something like 80 per cent of all living things. If true that is an extraordinary fact of this amazing planet. Diving beneath the surface of water, whether into the harbour or under a breaking wave in a powerful surf, seems to hold a sense of diving into the wonder and mystery of life itself. For the little boy who surrendered his rubber ring all those many years ago, it has ever been thus.

JOHN MCSWEENEY

Showing off at Brighton Baths

John McSweeney is a Brighton boy through and through. Apart from five years when he worked as a teacher in regional Victoria, he has lived in this bayside suburb of Melbourne since he was born at the Brighton Community Hospital in 1941. A key place in his childhood was the Brighton Baths, sometimes called the Middle Brighton Baths, a fixture on Port Phillip Bay since 1881 and rebuilt in 1936 and 1986. John has been swimming there since he was a small child.

My first visit to the Brighton Baths, or 'the baths' as we used to call them, was when I was four or five with my mum and dad and my brother and sister. It was the place we went every summer because it was a safe, enclosed and supervised area. Early on my parents took me there but by the time I was nine or so they'd let me go on my own. I'd get on my bike in the morning with the threepence entrance fee in my pocket and I'd be there for the day. I probably took a sandwich for lunch and I'd get home about half-past five.

There were no suburban pools back in the 1940s and 50s, and buses would bring kids all the way from Bentleigh, four or five kilometres away, and from Oakleigh, six kilometres away, and drop them right near the baths. Often on hot days there would be a queue up to 50 or 100 metres long of kids waiting to get in. We got to know all those kids who came from other suburbs. Everyone knew everyone at the baths and the big kids looked after the little kids.

The baths were like entering the womb because you'd go in through the entrance, down this little passageway, and then you'd come out into this big watery area. The water in the baths is a lot shallower now than it was when I was a kid as all this sand has come in. There's tons of it and we don't know where it's come from. A timber boardwalk about 440 yards long surrounded the water and there were ladders at different spots to climb in and out. It was 55 yards in width and 110 yards from the shallows to the deep end, so if you swam in a circuit it was about 330 yards.

The change rooms used to be outdoors and had no roof on them, which was pretty interesting on the colder days, and the water didn't really get swimmable until late November or early December. You could swim comfortably up until Easter, and then it got pretty cold again. The temperature rose to about 22 degrees and on rare occasions maybe 24, and then dropped down to as low as eight degrees in the winter. In the past few years I've become an all-year-round swimmer at the baths, but when I was a kid I only swam in the summertime. We thought the place was wonderful and on hot nights it was adorned with lights so you could stay there till eight or nine o'clock at night.

It was monitored by a manager in residence and he had a house upstairs. He was a council employee and his name was Tim Jones. He gave me a job at the kiosk selling lollies, ice creams and drinks a few days a week in the summer holidays and I made a bit of pocket money, which was good. Tim Jones ran a very tight ship. If there was an altercation between boys he would grab them and put boxing gloves on them and say, 'Go for it,' until it was sorted. Everyone formed a great big ring and cheered them on. If any children misbehaved or were reported to be misbehaving, Tim would frogmarch them from one end of the baths to the other, gather up their clothes and put them out. He'd tell them they couldn't return unless they came back with their mum or dad.

On the odd occasion there'd be a jellyfish in the water – a big round one with a cross on its head like a hot cross bun – and every now and again a stingray would get in (apparently they can turn sideways). There was always lots of fish, and mussels grew on the steel bars around the bottom of the baths that kept out the sharks. Tim Jones made quite a good living out of collecting bags of mussels and selling them.

When I was there as a young fella I used to play all sorts of games – chasey, duck diving for things on the bottom, and swimming all the time, round and round. There were three diving boards, including two that we would now call one-metre boards, and one three-metre board, and they were flat out all day with kids leaping off them. There was a slide that you slid down from the boardwalk into the water at rapid speed, and there was a wheel you ran on, which would get faster and faster until your legs couldn't keep up and you fell in.

The *Herald* Learn to Swim campaign was held at the baths. It was sponsored by the newspaper and staffed by volunteers who taught once or twice a week for free. There'd be 15 or 20 kids in a swimming lesson and when you were deemed to be competent you were asked to swim 25 yards in order to gain *The Herald* Learn to Swim certificate. I always loved swimming and was pretty good at it, so I got one of those certificates, but even the kids who couldn't swim got one as it was held down the shallow end and they just ran along the bottom.

There was a swimming club at the baths every Sunday morning with all the under-age competitions in the three strokes: backstroke, breaststroke and freestyle. I was a member of the club until I was about 14. Most of us left around that age and went to join the Brighton Life Saving Club because that's where the girls were. The club races were held whether it was raining or blowing a gale and it was all run by volunteer parents. There were seniors right down to Under 10s, and once a year we would have an annual competition swim against the Brighton Beach Swimming Club. It alternated, one year at our baths and the next year at Brighton Beach. It was called the Ham Cup after a well-known family in Brighton Beach.

I taught myself to dive on the boards at the baths. There were a couple of older kids who were really good and I used to copy them. I got the somersault going and I thought I was doing really well and then I saw them mocking me one day because instead of pointing my toes I looked like I had boots on. They were pointing at me pulling their knees up in the tuck position with their boots on and laughing. I thought, *Oh I see – you've got to point your toes*. So, I learned like that. In the juniors you only had to do three dives. Standing straight, like a swallow dive, a running swallow dive, and then one dive of your own choice, and I was absolutely sensational at doing a one-and-a-half somersault in the pike position.

When I was competing in the Under 13s at the Victorian diving championships I came third off the one-metre board and afterwards about five people were lined up to see if they could be my coach. Money was pretty bloody tight as my dad was a railway worker and he said we just couldn't afford it. So they all backed off and then this chap wandered over to Dad and had a chat and both of them came back to me and he said, 'Be at the Olympic Pool, Tuesday afternoon after school.' His name was Alan Mott and he offered to coach me for free.

He was a previous Australian springboard diving champion and he coached me for two years. In that period I was Victorian champion in the Under 14s, Under 15s and Under 16s. I've always felt I didn't really acknowledge that bloke enough, but I was only a kid. I used to rock up twice a week to the old Olympic Pool on Batman Avenue that was later named the Beaurepaire Centre after Frank Beaurepaire, a champion swimmer and former mayor of Melbourne. I'd dive for an hour on the boards at that pool, which were as good as you could get at the time. They were quite springy and had a sort of sandpaper-type surface so you didn't slip. They were very different to the board I dived off at the Brighton Baths, which was a big lump of wood with a hessian bag around it to stop you slipping. And I was diving into chlorinated water, not salt.

I was a bit of a show-off and the higher I went the better, so I adapted to diving off those springy boards at the old Olympic Pool and the even better ones at the Olympic pool built for the 1956 Olympics, the venue where I won the Under 15s and Under 16s Victorian championships. Under Alan Mott I didn't get beaten for those three years, but I didn't dive after the Under 16s. Once I got to seniors I had to learn six more dives that involved twists and more turns. I was born with a slow twitch muscle, so I was very graceful, but not very quick. I couldn't complete those dives in the allotted times so I crashed a hell of a lot and in the end I said, 'I can't do it because I'm just not built for it.' I gave up diving competitively but continued diving for fun back on those old planks at the baths.

The Brighton Baths were colossal fun when I

was a kid and a great meeting place. Everything about them was such a pleasure – the whole set up and all the kids and groups you'd meet from every school around. I still swim there now and there's still a fabulous community of people. If you need looking after, it's there. There's teachers, there's lawyers, there's physios, there's former policemen, there's osteopaths. We've got the whole thing covered.

I always say it's a place where nobody matters but everybody matters – you can be the judge of the county court or you can be the local garbage man and no one would have a clue when they're all down there because they all mix and mingle. The Brighton Baths are my spiritual home. I said to my daughter, 'When I die …' and she said, 'I know, we'll go and spread your ashes over the baths.'

THERESE SPRUHAN

Embracing the glorious king tide

I spent my childhood in the 1960s and 70s in Northbridge, on Sydney's lower north shore. As a toddler I joined my two siblings in the family's canvas wading pool in the backyard of our Californian bungalow. One year that wading pool was packed away and never seen again. By then, I had moved on to deeper water at Northbridge Baths, an expansive tidal enclosure that has been part of Sailors Bay, a tranquil corner of Middle Harbour, since 1924.

My earliest memory of Northbridge Baths is a flash of movement and the colour pink. It is late 1964, and I am four. Mum has just applied pink zinc to my nose and shoulders on the grassed area at the baths where my family always sat when we were little. Then I am running towards the water in my stretchy pale pink one-piece, past my little brother Mark playing with his bucket and spade on the sand, and towards Dad in the olive-green water.

I climb on his back and he takes me out to the deeper part where the water turns a darker emerald. He pretends to be a crocodile about to eat me up and I giggle when he turns his head and opens his mouth as if he is about to take a bite. When we head back to the shallows my older sister Annette has a go on Dad's back and then Mum joins us in the water, holding my hands and leading me along, encouraging me to blow bubbles and kick. Later, when Mum calls out that it's time to leave, I duck under again so I will take home the feel of the water and the smell of salt on my skin.

Soon after that memory, when I was still four, I went to my first official swimming lessons, but they were at the Lane Cove pool, not Northbridge Baths, and I wasn't happy. I didn't like the way the chlorine went down the back of my nose when I floated or attempted to do backstroke. I was happy the following year when my lessons were back in the salt water at the baths. Each year we did 'Learn to Swim' classes and extra ones with Col, the tall, tanned-like-leather manager of the baths, and on 26 January 1968, when I was seven, I was awarded a certificate signed by H Wyndham, the Director-General of the NSW Department of Education, for swimming 30 yards.

Eighteen months later, on the first Saturday in October 1969, Mum drove my sister and brother and me down to the baths to join the Northbridge Amateur Swimming Club. After that, my relationship with the baths became very tied up with the swimming club. For the next 10 years my Saturday morning routine in summer started before 7 a.m. when my sister and I got up, put on our Speedos, T-shirts and a pair of terry-towelling shorts. We'd wrap our towels around our necks and step into thongs and try not to wake our parents as we shut the front door. Then we'd walk around to our neighbours, the Halls, and when our friends Therese and Kathleen emerged we'd head down their side steps and onto Minnamurra Road. From there it was all downhill, and if we were late, we'd run. Halfway along Widgiewa Road, the very steep street that led down to the baths, we'd take a short cut through the bush and emerge in the car park, where a kookaburra would be letting out a loud *who, who, ha, ha* in one of the twisting pink-orange angophoras as a blue-tongue lizard slithered across our path. Then we'd bound down the steps, hand Col our 20 cents, push through the turnstiles and we were in.

On the concrete area in front of the men's change rooms, bodies with that just-out-of-bed smell in different stages of undress would be milling around card tables signing on for the morning's races. Most Saturdays I entered the 50-metre events in all strokes and on alternate weeks I'd do a 200-metre freestyle or 200-metre medley, and once a year the club held a mile swim which involved 32 laps. After we'd signed on for our races we'd walk around to the deep end to stake out a spot on the bench above the boardwalk. The orange and white lane ropes would be unrolled and attached to eight chrome hooks at the bottom of the blocks at each end of the 50-metre area.

'Last call for entries,' would come over the PA as the club organisers made their way around to the deep end with their clipboards.

When my first race was called I'd pull my cap over my head and jump down onto the blocks, which could be quite a leap if the tide was low, and one time I remember I hurt my foot when I landed hard. There was a ladder not far away, but only little kids and older people took that route. When everyone was standing in front of their lane, the starter would call out, 'On your mark, get set,' and after the gun went off, he'd count out from one in a loud voice, to sometimes into the 20s, as the races were all handicap events.

It was hard to swim straight in the lanes and often I'd veer too much to the right and my arm would crash into the rope or a jelly blubber. I'd straighten up again and when my hand touched the blocks at the other end, the timekeeper, who would be one of the parents in a floppy hat, old T-shirt and Speedos, would lean down and call out my time. I'd swim under the lane ropes and climb up the chrome ladder shining silver in the sun and re-join my sister and my friends on the bench.

After the races were over and the lane ropes were pulled in, I'd go to the shop and buy my lollies. Col would be standing behind the counter in his navy Speedos that he wore low on his bum and when I'd walk up to the counter he'd say, 'Yes, Therese.' Col could never pro-nounce my name the same as everyone else. He always made it rhyme with cerise in a way that made it sound more exotic. 'Two Redskins, one Spearmint, one Milko, a Raspberry Pop, and a Curl,' I would say and he'd drop them into a small white paper bag and take my 20 cents.

Then I'd start my journey home, unwrapping one of my Redskins and sucking on it as I trudged back up the very steep Widgiewa Road and wound my way up Minimbah and Minnamurra Roads till I reached our house in Byora Crescent. When I got home, I'd go to my room and lie on my bed. The smell of grass being mowed would waft through my open window and another kookaburra that lived in the huge gum tree next door would laugh. I'd lie back on my bed with my lollies and daydream, enjoying the blissful feeling in my body after a morning of hard exercise.

Other times I went to the baths just to swim, not to race or compete. During the summer in primary school I'd walk down there almost every afternoon after school, always wanting to be in that water. Sometimes my sister and brother came with me, or I met my friends, but if they weren't around I went on my own. When I was really little I didn't mind if the tide was low, but once I could swim, I always wished for high tide. At low tide the water seemed heavier, and there was half the space to swim in. When it was high, the entire area inside the shark-proof fence was covered in water and the beach in the shallows was submerged.

The state of the tides determined whether Mum and Dad came for a swim, and the tide tables printed at the back of the *Sydney Morning Herald* were regularly consulted.

When we called out the time the high tide was due, that's when they'd go for a swim. Mum was a keener swimmer than Dad, but high tide could lure him to the baths at sometimes not very convenient times, like Christmas morning when all hands were meant to be on deck to prepare for lunch with our cousins. That tradition of a Christmas morning swim didn't last long as Mum was never impressed when Dad, with us three in tow, headed down to the baths and left her with all the work.

Most of the time I was at the baths with my siblings and friends, but some of my strongest memories are of being there with my parents at special times, like when the king tide flowed in. It only happened once or twice a season, and on those days the baths were at their best. The water changed from green to blue and was almost crystal clear. Every corner was filled to the brim, spilling over the tops of the blocks and the concrete steps in the shallows. Everyone flocked to the baths at king tide, but I can only picture my family lit up in the foreground: Mum is swimming a lap in her light blue cossie with the skirt panel over the top and her matching latex cap. She's swimming with her high arm-lifting style like she's reaching over a wave, the result of learning to swim in the surf at Maroubra Beach and in the swell of Wylie's Baths. When she gets to the end, she says 'Lovely,' out loud. 'It's so lovely in,' she repeats and turns on her back and floats.

Dad is there too, launching himself into the water from the shallows and following his usual routine of swimming about 10 strokes of flat-arm freestyle and then switching to breaststroke with his head on the side, a technique we always thought was a bit odd, like his ambidextrous tennis style. My sister and brother and I jump off the concrete boardwalk and swim across to our parents and we try to climb on Dad's back like when we were little kids, not children of 10, 12 and 13. As we grab hold of him, he starts laughing and drowning at the same time and as usual gets a cramp. We swim across to the blocks and as Dad stretches his foot, he joins Mum, waxing lyrical about the beauty of the baths today. 'Glorious,' he says as he works out his cramp. When the tide starts to go out, we go to the shop for a treat, which today isn't the usual lemonade icy pole or chocolate Paddle-Pop. It's a Pine-Lime Splice, a Triple Treat or a Golden Gaytime!

On other days, the water at the deep end of the baths was quite dark. When my brother was little he was scared of the dense water and he'd only get in after Mum gently coaxed him. My sister and I weren't scared of the dark water or of the slippery jellyfish that floated in, and when hordes of them invaded the water we had fun throwing them at each other. We also weren't scared of the occasional stingray that used to float into the shallow area and hover near an oyster-crusted concrete pylon under the boardwalk. But we were scared of the maroon-brown man-of-war jellyfish that occasionally drifted in from the open water in Sailors Bay.

Every now and again one appeared in the middle of a lane during the swimming club events on Saturday mornings. Once it was spotted, the races were stopped and someone would run and get Col to come around to the deep end with his net with the very long pole. Everyone would leave the water and quiet would descend over the baths, like at the beach when there's a shark alarm. When Col scooped up the stinging jellyfish and threw it over the fence into Sailors Bay, we'd all cheer. A few minutes later the races would start again, but as I swam I'd shut my eyes to stop images of red-brown jellyfish appearing in the water in front of me.

Everyone had their favourite spots at the baths. Families congregated on the grassed area near the shallows; my friends and I would try to avoid stepping on the prickly bindi-eyes there as we ran across. Ernie, a local postman, waded through the shallows early in the morning before his shift and fed bread to the fish – mullet, blackfish, garfish and bream. Our next-door neighbour, Aunty Helen, who had Nazi concentration camp numbers on her forearm, always headed to the deep end, where she swam a slow breaststroke up and down. I had a few favourite spots: an area in the middle of the baths that was just the right depth for our handstand competitions (though we had to be careful to avoid sharp rocks), the bench on the boardwalk where I hung out on Saturday mornings with all the girls, and the blocks I dived off at the start of a race.

The blocks were like a rectangular slab of ice that floated on the water at either end of the 50-metre swimming area. They were white fibreglass and across the front were numbers in black from one to eight. Affixed to them were the horizontal chrome handles we held onto at the start of our backstroke races. If the blocks hadn't been cleaned for a while the underwater part would be covered in green slime, so when you held on to the handles and put your feet on the blocks, your feet would often slip. A whole group of us girls often used to gather by the blocks after the races on Saturday or at other times on the weekend. One by one my friends would duck-dive under the blocks and come up on the other side, under the boardwalk. I'd watch Kathleen do it numerous times and see the excitement she felt when she emerged on the other side. I'd duck-dive under but never went very far as I was always worried about getting stuck or where I might end up in that murky, mysterious underneath world.

Every now and again my friends and I used to leap off the pale blue diving board that was in a separate area on one side of the baths, but most of the time it was occupied by the tough boys. They wore boardshorts, not Speedos like the males in the swimming club, and smoked cigarettes and pashed off with their girlfriends lying on their towels on the concrete area next to the board. My friends and I would watch their exploits – usually competitions to see who could do the biggest bomb and get closest to the concrete wall without hitting it. I can still hear the sound of that board going *booongg, boonnggg, booongg* as they bounced up and down and then that final double *booongg* when they leapt off, leaning their body backwards and holding on to one leg. And then there was the enormous splash rising above the concrete and wetting their girlfriends, who lay in the sun in their 1970s crocheted bikinis. Once, one of the boys went too close and hit his leg on the concrete wall. He surfaced with blood pouring down his leg and unable to climb back up the ladder, and someone had to run for Col.

Col was a major presence at the baths. He mostly stayed in the area behind the shop and only emerged when he was needed to take swimming lessons, coach water polo or clean the bottom of the blocks. He very rarely went in the water, but when he did we were impressed by his languid, effortless swimming style. Only occasionally did he raise his voice when someone was really playing up or if a few of the boys got in a fight. A lot of the time he walked very slowly around the boardwalk with a sort of swagger, in his white thongs and navy Speedos. We knew he was married and lived somewhere in the south side of Sydney, maybe near Cronulla, and occasionally he brought his son, who had an intellectual disability, to the baths. But Col was always a bit of a mystery to us kids. He was probably the same age as my mother, but a bit cooler, and I think he might have smoked cigarettes. It always made me happy when he said I'd done a good time in a race.

When I was 15, I became a senior at the club. This meant I competed against anyone over that age, male or female. Next to me on the blocks could be a few girls from my water polo team, a local electrician who was the president of the club, one of the suburb's GPs, and the handsome father of the children I had just started to babysit. I liked the challenge of racing against men and it spurred me on to swim as fast as I could. But I wasn't climbing on boys' shoulders like some of my friends, or lying close on the grass and pashing off with them. I preferred the romantic fantasies in my head of completely unattainable men, like a tall, blond, handsome guy in the club called Roly, who was about 23, or James Brolin, aka Dr Steve Kiley on *Marcus Welby MD* on TV.

The biggest day at the baths was the club championships, which was always held on the last Sunday in March. Around 2 p.m. Mum and Dad and all the other parents would take their places on the bench where my friends and I usually sat on Saturday mornings. It was the one day of the season that Mum and Dad came to the swimming club. They were never ones to get overexcited about winning – their mantra was more about doing your best. If I arrived back at their spot after winning a race, their reaction was usually very low-key. You never wanted to take yourself too seriously or show off.

What my father enjoyed most about those championship days was stirring my sister and me that he was going to put our names down for the father-daughter race. Each year when an announcement came over the PA calling for last entries, he'd start his spiel – *Quick we'd better go and put our names down.* And each year we'd both reply with a very adamant *No!* As far as my sister and I were concerned, Dad's swimming ability was not up to competing in the father-daughter race. When he was about 10 he'd taken part in a week of lessons at Sydney's Domain Baths, where the key instruction was, 'Jump in, sonny, and get to there,' which he duly did, and after thrashing about he reached the other side. Since then his swimming ability had only developed slightly, so we were not keen for him to enter the father-daughter race. The other drawback was he wore trunks, not Speedos. Eventually he'd drop the idea after he'd had enough fun getting a reaction from us.

Occasionally we had to stay away from the baths when heavy rain fell and stormwater raced down the gully and polluted the pool. It was torture not being able to run down the hill and swim, but eventually we'd get word that the council had given the all-clear and we could get back in the water. Around Easter time when the baths closed for winter I'd always feel a bit sad, but we didn't get a winter key like our next-door neighbour Aunty Helen, who swam all year round. The baths were our summer place and in winter netball and rugby took over our Saturday mornings. Then before we knew it, October would arrive and it would be time for the swimming club again.

Over the past 30 or so years since I moved away from Northbridge, every now and again I've returned to the baths for a swim. But when my father died in 2006, 14 years after my mother, there wasn't much reason to head north over the Sydney Harbour Bridge. I connected to other pools near where I lived in the inner west. But the baths never left me, and when I started to think about writing about them, all sorts of memories came flooding back – from the zing of a Whizz Fizz on my tongue to the sweet sound of the butcher birds swooping over the water, jacaranda flowers poking through the eucalypts on the headlands above the baths and the smell of salt water mixed with the sweet fragrance of the bush.

But most of all I remembered the baths through the feel of the surfaces on my hands and my feet – the roughness of the blocks, the slimy jellyfish, the coarse sand gathering around my hands when I dived under and did a handstand, the embrace of the salt water as I floated, and always the joy of being there with my family when the glorious king tide flowed in.

Sea pools

LIZZIE BUCKMASTER DOVE

Falling in love with the Blue Pool

Five months before Lizzie Buckmaster Dove turned 12, she travelled to Bermagui on the far south coast of New South Wales from her home in outback Lightning Ridge nearly 1000 kilometres away. Her mother and one of her older brothers were with her and on the second day of their week-long holiday they went to the Blue Pool, developed in the late 1930s out of the Blue Hole at the bottom of a cliff next to the Tasman Sea.

The first time I saw the Blue Pool was in the January summer holidays in 1982 when I was 11. I had never seen a sea pool before and when I looked down on it from the cliff above, it was like this incomprehensible vision. I couldn't make sense of it, suspended on the side of a headland leading into the sea.

It was about 40 metres long and perhaps nearly 15 metres at the widest point, but it wasn't an even, rectangular-shaped pool. It curved into the side of a honey-coloured cliff, and near the sea parts of the rockface jutted into the pool and waves washed over the edge. The colour of the water was a brilliant blue and looking at this vision of a body of water right next to the sea was mind-blowing.

In the early part of my life, when I lived on an orchard in the foothills of Victoria's Dandenong Ranges, we had holidays at the coast, but when I was six my parents separated and my life became very inland. We moved first to Wee Waa in north-west New South Wales to be near my mother's parents, then to Dubbo for two years, and then to the opal-mining town of Lightning Ridge for five years, where I swam in waterholes, dams and at the bore baths. When we visited my mother's parents at Yarrawonga in Victoria, where they settled after Wee Waa, we spent all day floating down the Murray River on tyres. All these watery places were surrounded by land, so the coast was a mysterious thing to me.

When I saw the Blue Pool, I felt I was in-between the land and the sea. It was magical, like I'd stepped through the wardrobe in Narnia into this lucid, liminal, watery world. That sense of the infinity of the ocean was just completely mesmerising and beside it was this pool, part-natural, part man-made, just waiting for me. That was the start of my love affair with the Blue Pool, but I didn't tell my mother or brother or anyone about the impact it had on me – that it made me feel like anything was possible. It was my secret.

My memories of that week at the Blue Pool are like little freeze-frames of swimming or being still at the side of the pool and looking out over the Tasman Sea. I always had a sketchbook with me when I was kid as I was drawing all the time and I had it with me at the pool. I remember very clearly sitting on the edge and being observed by a man as I did a drawing of my goggles and snorkel with my 2B pencil. It wasn't an awful feeling or overly sexual, but at some point he said, 'That's a really good drawing.' I was wanting to impress him and I was impressed that I was impressive. My almost-12-year-old sense of my sexual self was just starting to blossom, and that moment encompassed all those feelings of being at this sensual place, the pool, and being aware of boys, of males. I was also rather pleased with my drawing.

When we left Bermagui, I took the Blue Pool with me. It lodged itself in my head and I carried the wonder of it around with me; the insane impossibility of sea pools. It lived in my head almost like a dreamscape and as time went on I felt I must have imagined it. The longer I was away from it, the more I thought it couldn't possibly exist. In my teenage years I didn't have any other experiences of being absolutely astounded by the existence of something as I did at the Blue Pool.

I was not blown away in that way again until I moved to Sydney in 1990 and met the Bronte ocean pool. That's when I found out that there were lots of sea pools dotted all up and down the New South Wales coast. I realised the Blue Pool wasn't a construct of my imagination. All that time between nearly the ages of 12 and 20, the Blue Pool was gestating in my mind, doing its watery thing, and then when I was 22 and at art school, it started to inform my work. Sea pools started entering my art and when I had a dancefloor-induced vision of six naked women diving into a sea pool with sequinned bathing caps, I took a group of friends to Wombarra Pool on the Illawarra coast. I photographed them at dawn and as they dived in they were like a blur of bodies and sequins on the edge of the water suspended in an in-between state.

When I look back over my life, I can see how much the Blue Pool has informed me. It's like the structure of me – the skeleton of me – like a double helix underneath all my art and why I live near a sea pool. When we moved to Coledale in 2007, I wouldn't have said that it was a sea pool that drew me there, but once I was there it seemed obvious that of course I would live in the Illawarra where there's such a high density of sea pools.

The Blue Pool was the start of my love affair with sea pools and since I saw it for the first time from the top of the cliff more than 30 years ago, it has inspired my passions in terms of making art and my fascination with liminal, in-between places and stages in life.

ASHLEY HAY

Reflections on the water at Austinmer

Ashley Hay spent her childhood at Austinmer on
the New South Wales Illawarra coast, an area
early settlers described as a poet's corner and a
bohemian paradise. In the 1970s and 80s her world
revolved around the bush tracks on the Illawarra
escarpment above her family's home. Her other
favourite place was Austinmer Beach, where she
spent many hours making imaginary cities out of
sand, riding her surfoplane and swimming in the
two magnificent ocean pools created out of the
southern rock platform in the 1920s and late 30s.

The earliest memory I have of the ocean pools is of
a lovely older man called Mr Luck, a local former
surf lifesaving champion, who used to teach people to
swim. I had lessons with him before I was old enough
to be at school. I remember very clearly the sensation of
the bottom of my foot pushing off from the knobbly, rocky

side of the pool and how different it felt compared to the tiles in the Olympic pool at nearby Thirroul. It was as if I could feel this place more because of its roughness.

The two pools had such distinct personalities. The northern one was the older of the two by more than 10 years. When the southern one was added in the late 1930s, it was built right next to the northern one and a concrete walkway connected the two. They were called double or twin ocean pools, but they were definitely not identical. The southern pool was a very different body of water to the northern one and I always loved watching who gravitated to one and who gravitated to the other. I always preferred the northern pool. It was wider, and because the sand often banked up at the shallow end I could just step off the wall and start walking along the bottom of the pool. The sides seemed a bit lower, which made it feel like the pool was still connected to the ocean. The southern pool was narrower and I could never guarantee how deep it was going to be, which felt very suspicious when I was a child.

I wasn't ever one of the brave kids who stood on the pools' back wall to get washed off. I wasn't a particularly strong swimmer and my overactive imagination meant I didn't like the idea of being swept off the edge and out to sea. That same imagination meant I spent quite some time looking – with great hope – for under-the-sea fairies like the ones that were in Peg Maltby's *Book of Fairies*, a picture book I loved. Sometimes there was seaweed and little fish and one day a wobbegong shark got in the pool. But I never found the under-the-sea fairies.

As a kid I didn't pay much attention to the tides, but it was exciting if I hit that sweet spot when whatever it was that I wanted to happen was happening – either the water in the pools was completely still and calm, or the waves were coming through to create that washing-machine feel. I loved it when the tide was in and there was surf in the pools and you could catch waves in an enclosed space.

My primary school, Austinmer Public, was across the road from the beach and some afternoons it felt like the whole class ended up in the pools. There would be a big lump of kids in the water. Sometimes we were bussed over to Thirroul pool for swimming lessons or a swimming carnival because it was a properly tiled 50-metre pool, not a rough-edged, sandy-bottomed sea pool. I was outraged that Thirroul was being preferred over Austinmer for these events; I think I took it personally on the pools' behalf. Thirroul was a saltwater pool but it seemed like an entirely different animal – all those tiles – and it seemed to me a kind of slight that we had to be shipped south to a 'proper pool' for our carnival.

My family were all-year-round beach people – not just in summer – and at some point in my childhood my parents started swimming at the pool each morning around six o'clock: first my dad, and then my mum as well. I used to go too and walk on the beach and sometimes I'd jump in for a swim. It was a beautiful way to set the rhythm of the day. It became habit; the particular way we walked around to the old cast concrete dressing sheds; the particular place we put our things; the particular walk down the steps and off across the sand towards the pools. It was an extraordinary place to start each day; the bodies of water were different every morning and the palette and light were always changing.

We got a new dog when I was 12 or 13, and we'd have dinner and then take her for a walk down to the beach; there were always beautiful reflections in the pools at night. Because of their rectangular shape, they looked like paintings. I love the American artist Mark Rothko's rectangular experiments with colour and the French painter Yves Klein's big panels of monochrome blue. Maybe these things come from the image of those pools.

Once, a friend and I walked up to the top of Sublime Point – the summit of the escarpment above Austinmer – and when we were coming down an amazing thunderstorm came in. We were completely drenched. My parents live at the bottom of the track to Sublime Point but we went straight past the house and kept going down the hill to jump in the pool. We were so wet that it seemed like the only sensible thing to do was to be even more wet again. There'd been so much water on top of us, it felt magical to be floating on more water still as the rain kept coming down. It was fantastic.

Austinmer is small – there's less than a kilometre of plain between the beach and the escarpment. When I was in the pools, I loved to swim to the back wall, turn around and look up at that mountain. It looked amazingly tall and imposing. And then one year I went on a boat trip from Circular Quay out through Sydney Heads

and down to Wollongong Harbour, and I saw the escarpment from out at sea for the first time. It seemed so much
bigger from out there, and it astonished me to realise it
was a much more looming, rising thing and that the pools
were just a tiny band of rock and water at the bottom. It
made the place that I'd always thought was special feel
even more momentous and, after that, looking out to the
horizon from the pools' edge, I always felt like I could
almost see the curve, and sense of the shape of, the world.

RICHARD CHMIELEWSKI

Diving for catches
in Adelaide

If Richard Chmielewski's parents hadn't bribed him with chocolate to keep him learning to swim, he might never have progressed from his teacher's backyard pool to Adelaide's Olympic-size Henley and Grange Pool. But persevere he did, thanks to his Polish-born parents who came to Australia as displaced persons after World War II and settled in the beachside suburb of Henley. From 1970, when nine-year-old Rick became a member of the Henley and Grange Swimming Club, the seawater pool became his favourite summer haunt.

Our house was on The Esplanade opposite Henley Beach and 300 metres from the Henley and Grange Olympic Pool. Living so close to the water, my parents felt it was imperative that we kids learned to swim, but I didn't learn at the age of two or three like they do now. I was seven or eight when I started lessons with Mr Renfrey, a local swimming instructor who taught us in his back-yard pool. I really hated those swimming lessons because Mr Renfrey was very strict.

At one point he would give us a directive to swim from one end of the pool to the other. So you'd hop in at the deep end and attempt to swim to the shallow end. If you were struggling a little you'd make your way to the side of the pool, but he would push you back to the centre with a broomstick. Some of the parents were outraged by this and said, 'Don't treat my child like that.' Mr Renfrey would respond, 'Well, if you don't like it, get out.' Most people took that on board because it was the era of more authoritarian-style teaching, whether it was for swimming or at school. He also had a great reputation for producing good swimmers and he taught probably 90 per cent of the children in the area.

I survived those lessons and learned to swim. Two years later, when I was about nine or 10, I started squad with Mr Renfrey in his 15-metre backyard pool. Around the same time I also became a member of the Henley and Grange Amateur Swimming Club, which was formed in 1912. Back then the club members trained and competed in the sea, but when the pool opened in 1934 they moved their Sunday morning races there.

The pool was unique as it was the only Olympic-size seawater pool in South Australia. It was built on the beach but elevated about three metres above the sand and the water was pumped in from the sea – the St Vincent Gulf. We thought it was wonderful but other swimming clubs we competed against every few weeks – Marion and Payneham, which had chlorine pools – hated the place. It was right on the seafront so it was very exposed to the weather. Early in the season in November, and in April just before the pool closed for winter, storms often came in when carnivals were on.

On The Esplanade side there was some seating for spectators, but most of it was on the sea side, where a chainmail fence and wooden slats provided no protection from the elements. Visiting parents watching their children swim came to realise they had to bring raincoats with them, otherwise they'd get wet from the spray from the waves. When the tide was high it flowed all the way up the beach to the base of the pool and the wind would whip up the water and soak the spectators. The water for the pool was pumped in from the sea so it could be quite cold, which the other clubs also didn't like, as the temperature never rose above 21 degrees.

None of that mattered to us as the pool was our playground, our meeting place away from any parental constraints. In the summer school holidays I went there every day and I'd get very annoyed if we had to visit my parents' friends and I couldn't go to the pool. At 10, I was well and truly over my early reluctance to swim. Now I loved it, not just because I enjoyed the physical activity of swimming but also because of the social and competitive aspects of the club. My training partners were my friends and we would all meet on Sunday mornings at the club races at the pool. I'd usually enter about half a dozen events, normally under the direction of Mr Renfrey, and in between races we'd socialise on the grassed area on The Esplanade side of the pool. We'd put our towels down and sit in circles and chat and only wander off when we had a race. There were boys and girls and over that five- or six-year period in the early to mid-1970s, I had a couple of girlfriends from the group. We would meet up on those Sunday mornings and maybe another day if they came to the pool.

My parents never came to the Sunday morning club races. Dad was a quantity surveyor working in the building industry and Mum ran shops – mainly delicatessens. They were both very hard workers and at the time I thought they were strict, but looking back I had a lot of free time to go to the pool, and I can't believe how spoilt I was. They were both doing very long hours, yet I didn't even have to do the dishes. They were good parents but I would have thought they were invading my territory if they came to the pool. But lots of the other parents were very involved in the swimming club. It was a social time for them as well as for us kids and they'd bring along sandwiches and cakes and make tea and coffee in the club room, and when the events were over they'd have a big morning tea. But on those Sunday mornings, the parents and the kids were very separate and the groups didn't venture into each other's space.

At the time the pool was built, it was Olympic standard with eight lanes, but there was no overflow, which meant there was a lot of movement in the water from all the bodies racing and you'd often bump into the lane ropes, which were just a rope with a cork every metre or so. In 1976, when I was 15, I was the club champion. I swam in all the races considered club championship events, but there were two other boys my age who were away at the states or nationals, so in a way I made it by default. If they had been there I would have been third in the club at the time.

Outside of those Sunday club mornings, I spent a lot of time just enjoying the atmosphere of the pool. On the really hot days we'd lounge around and bake ourselves in the sun. There was no sunscreen back then but there was coconut oil, which you'd lather yourself in and lie and sunbake until you were virtually black. I had some terrible sunburn but I was better off than many because I have olive skin from my parents. When we got too hot we'd jump back in the water to cool off.

The inside of the pool was painted a sea-blue colour and the water was very clear because a filter stopped any sand coming in and you could always see to the bottom. Occasionally we had marine life in the pool that didn't come in via the pump. About 50 metres from the pool was the Henley Jetty, and like all the jetties in South Australia it attracted a lot of fishermen. On their way home some of the fishermen would drop the catch they didn't want into the pool. Sometimes we'd have fish and crabs swimming around and one day they dumped a shark in the pool. The manager wanted us boys to get in and move it towards the shallows so they could get it out, but we weren't keen. We didn't know it was a pretty harmless species of shark so we resisted for quite a while. Eventually we got in and there were three or four of us splashing around trying to direct it towards the shallows.

On hot days there would be several hundred people at the pool, but some of my fondest memories are of the colder months at the beginning of each season and towards the end of April when there'd be hardly anyone there. We had a core group of about five of us that went to the pool – me, my two brothers and two close friends – and we made friends with the manager/lifeguard, who was a young guy of about 30. He let us work in the kiosk and take people's money while he did chores around the pool. Our payment was in lollies – Redskins, milk bottles, snakes, bananas, red and green frogs and the South Australian brand of ice cream, AMSCOL – the Adelaide Milk Supply Cooperative Limited.

On the really cold days when no one was at the pool we'd go downstairs to the club room, which was the original one built back in the mid-1930s, and play cards and board games like Monopoly with the manager. The manager taught us to play poker and 21 and we used matchsticks to bet. It was the same space where the swimming club parents prepared their morning teas, but on those cold mornings we had it all to ourselves. If we got sick of playing cards and board games and the wind wasn't howling we'd go upstairs and play a version of backyard cricket on the bitumen area next to the pool.

The bitumen area was our cricket pitch, and if you hit the ball in one direction it would go towards the grassed area and the fence, and in the other direction it would go towards the pool. It was always best to hit it towards the water as that gave the players the opportunity to leap into the pool and try and catch the ball. It was wonderful fun taking diving catches in the water, and we'd spend hours and hours playing completely undisturbed by the general public. It was annoying when somebody wanted to come into the pool because it interrupted our game, and if there was a crowd the manager didn't let us play.

When the pool was first built it had a 30-foot diving tower, the equivalent of today's 10-metre tower, but it was gone by the time I was swimming there. In a particularly bad storm the base of the pool was damaged, causing a major leak. The most inexpensive way to repair it was to put more concrete in the bottom of the pool. This reduced the depth of the water under the tower to less than the original four metres, so they couldn't have the tower. But two one-metre springboards were still there in my era.

It was wonderful to use the springboards, and like a lot of boys we used to do bombs. In South Australia we called them storkies and sewies. A storkie involved leaping off the diving board and grabbing one leg so you looked a bit like a stork, and as you entered the water you slid backwards, creating the splash. A sewie was more like a dive, but as you entered the water you'd roll, and that would create a vertical splash of water. Some people could make it splash 20 or 30 feet into the air, so the higher you could make it go, the more esteem you were held in. We spent hours on the springboard, and once it was removed – no doubt for safety reasons – we'd do the same thing off the blocks at the deep end. The blocks were painted the same sea-blue colour as the inside of the pool.

A few of those blocks are now all that remains of the pool. They are part of a small memorial built next to the new Henley Surf Life Saving Club that replaced the old one and the pool building, including the club room where we played cards on cold days. I was still swimming at the pool after I joined the air force at 16 in 1977, and there was talk then that the council was going to close it down. People like me who loved the pool hoped its uniqueness would ensure its survival.

Sadly, that didn't happen. In 1985, when I was living in Sydney, I was devastated to hear it had been demolished. I felt a great sense of loss because I would never be able to revisit any of my treasured memories and I didn't get to have one last swim. I felt like something was taken from me; the Henley and Grange Pool was my favourite place in those years from the ages of nine through to 16. I still feel its loss today and I will always look back on those days with great fondness; picturing our core group leaping into the pool to take a catch at one of our endless cricket games always brings a smile to my face.

LINDA KENNEDY

Living it up at the Hollywood Pool

From 1968 to 1972, when Linda Kennedy was aged between seven and 11, she left suburban Adelaide behind to spend her summer holidays with her parents, six brothers and sisters, aunt and uncle and seven cousins camping at Foul Bay on South Australia's Yorke Peninsula. For those six weeks, her family of nine slept in sleeping bags in a large army tent with a layer of seaweed and plastic for their beds and fish, kangaroos, rabbits and pigeons caught by her father and uncle for their evening meals. They left the campsite once a week to go to mass, and when it was boiling hot they went to swim at a rock pool the family called the Hollywood Pool.

When the temperature climbed into the high 30s and 40s at our campsite at Foul Bay, it could be quite oppressive as there was no breeze, but at the Hollywood Pool it could be 10 degrees cooler. On those really hot days the adults would pack us all up and we'd head to the pool with all the kids in my family wearing a home-made rash shirt over our bathers with matching floppy hat that Mum had made out of old nylon dresses she had worn in the 1950s. Mum had seven kids in nine years and she was the original up-cycler and an early creator of the rash shirt. She also made a face-mask out of an old sheet for one of Aunty Mary's children who was very fair and kept getting sunburnt.

The Hollywood Pool was just south of Foul Bay in Investigator Strait, a body of water that lies between the peninsula and Kangaroo Island. The strait was named by the explorer Matthew Flinders when his ship HMS *Investigator* sailed by there in 1802. I imagine the Narungga Aboriginal people, the traditional owners of the peninsula, would have swum at the pool as it was a safe spot on that notoriously wild coast where many ships have been wrecked.

We were introduced to the pool by Uncle Noel and Aunty Mary, who was Dad's first cousin. They were wheat farmers near Yorketown on the peninsula and it was Uncle Noel who named the pool. He used to say, 'Every-one thinks that only people in Hollywood have pools but we've got our own Hollywood pool.' So that's what we always called it and as far as we were concerned, it was better than any glamorous backyard pool in Hollywood.

It was a real adventure getting to the pool. We'd all load into Uncle Noel's Land Rover, no seatbelts, no child restraints, with the windows down breathing in all the dust from the dirt road. We'd pass kangaroos bounding across the track in front of us and along the way there were farm gates to open and shut and we'd all fight over who'd jump out to open the gates. When we got to the top of the cliff, we'd unload the car and everyone would be given something to carry – eskies full of water and fruit, usually watermelon and Aunty Mary's kangaroo patties, and bags full of bread, and the older ones would have to help the little ones.

When we first went to the pool, my youngest brother Simon was one and a half, my littlest sister Joanna was two and a half, and Aunty Mary had a couple of little ones too. Mum or the older kids would carry a little one on their hip or on their back along the first part of the track, which was so narrow we had to walk in single file. I remember thinking I'd better not lose my footing because if I do I'll slide down the hill and crash onto the rocks. The next part of the journey was a steep area of soft sand, and if you got a run on you wouldn't be able to stop till you reached the beach at the bottom. Then we'd walk across a section of the beach and on to the rocks, which we'd skip over at a ridiculous speed, racing each other to the pool to be the first one in. When the rocks were hot we skimmed across even faster to prevent our feet from being burnt. It was always a relief when we reached the spot where the water flowed over the rocks and cooled them down.

When we finally reached the Hollywood Pool it felt like we were on the edge of the earth and we were the last people left on the planet. The fact that nobody else ever came there made it our secret place. It was an elongated circle surrounded by layers of beautiful rocks in pink-brown, pale orange and creamy-grey colours. It was wonderful not having to share it with anyone else except our two families, but it wasn't very big, so once you had 14 kids in there and the adults as well it was quite squishy.

Sometimes the water in the pool was completely still, but that didn't last for long as soon waves would wash over the rocks on the sea side and spill into the pool. The water was a beautiful blue-green with swirly patterns of white when the waves tumbled in. It often felt like you were swimming in a fish tank because you'd feel fish touch your legs as they swam by. Sometimes we wore masks or we'd open our eyes under the water and see big orange crabs with red or black dots on their back, or fish that would get caught in there. We'd swim around and hold our breath as long as we could and try to catch the fish, but we never did.

When it was a bit rough, we'd swim to the sea side of the pool and let the waves wash us back to the other side of the pool. We'd do it for hours or climb onto the rocks at the edge and let the force of the wave knock us into the pool. We never got tired of it, but it's a wonder that none of us got washed out into Investigator Strait. We never thought the water was cold, but it would have been as the current doesn't warm up much on that southern stretch of the coast.

It was an amazing adventure pool, so different to my

swimming experiences in suburban Adelaide where I had lessons at the Ethelton pool, your standard rectangular chlorine pool – long gone now. We literally marched there from our convent school and did our swimming lessons no matter what the weather. We also swam at Semaphore Beach, just down the road from our family home, where the water was sometimes clear and sometimes not. The water in the Hollywood Pool was always crystal clear, and being in it was wild, wonderful and exciting.

But we didn't stay in the water the whole time. We explored among the rocks around the pool and found crabs and creatures and sea anemones that squeezed up when you poked your finger in them. We spent quite a lot of time trying to figure out if there were fossils in the rocks. And seeing plants growing out of a tiny little crack in a rock that was battered by waves and the elements always amazed me.

I was an avid shell collector and one time when I was crawling all around the rocks I found a shell called a paper nautilus that is usually really difficult to find. It was quite a decent sized one jammed under a large rock, and when I first saw it I wasn't sure if it was intact. It took me some time to cautiously pry it from the rock, all the while pleading for it not to break. I remember running back to Mum and Dad yelling, 'Oh my God, I found one.' I was breathless with excitement. At that age I dreamed of being a marine biologist and I thought I was the luckiest child on the planet to find that paper nautilus. Fifty years later I still have it and it still brings me the same joy.

We also used to climb to the top of the high rocks on one side of the pool and my skinny brothers would jump off into the middle of the pool, which was probably only about seven feet deep. I wasn't the bravest so I left that stunt to my brothers, but I climbed to the top of the rockface many times. We were like little mountain goats and we'd scurry up there and scurry down to the bottom a dozen times and nobody ever fell over. Sometimes we'd climb over to the bay on the other side and no one ever worried where we were. They knew we'd come back when we were hungry.

My youngest sister, Joanna, who we called Joey, didn't like the water as much as everyone else. The first time we visited the Hollywood Pool she discovered an indentation in one of the large rocks near the pool which was almost a metre high but tapered off to only 30 centimetres or so at the back. She spent most of the time we were at the pool snug inside there, and so we called it Joey's Cave. She could sit in there and watch everything going on around her. Now if I tell her I've been down to the Hollywood Pool, she'll say 'Is my cave still there?'

There were times when it could get quite wild at the pool but I think that being fishermen, Dad and Uncle Noel worked out when it was a good day to go to there. Dad was like the original Steve Irwin. He was a big tease and a great storyteller too, but most of all he was really connected to the natural world and loved nothing more than taking his family on outdoor adventures. On those really hot days when I'd be begging him to go to the

Hollywood Pool, he would know if the tide was too high or if the wind was blowing in the wrong direction and he'd tell me I had to wait till the next day when the conditions would be better. On those days when we couldn't go to the Hollywood Pool, we'd explore Foul Bay. One evening when we were swimming quite late in an area where there was a reef, a large shark came right in next to us and we all had to jump out onto the reef and run across the top of it with no shoes on.

At the end of those six weeks camping out in the wilderness, living off the land and swimming at the Hollywood Pool, we'd return to Adelaide. For all that time we didn't wash our hair and I remember mine was stiff from salt, and we'd be as brown as berries. When we went back to school I'd try and tell the other kids stories about what we did and how we lived but none of them would believe me. We thought everybody had adventurous holidays like us, but when we'd tell them about eating kangaroo for dinner or swimming at a remote rock pool they thought we were making it up.

So I stopped trying to tell my friends what I'd done in the summer holidays, and then in 1972, when I was 11, nearly 12, our camping trips to Foul Bay abruptly ended. The council got wind that we'd been camping there, and it must not have been an official camping area, as from then on those carefree summers and adventures at the Hollywood Pool stopped.

It was a tragedy. I didn't go back to Foul Bay and I didn't get to swim at the Hollywood Pool again until quite recently, when my partner and I bought a house at Edithburgh, about an hour's drive from the pool. In those intervening years I didn't forget the Hollywood Pool; it remained a vivid memory of a wonderful time. When I wanted to picture something happy and beautiful in my head, I'd imagine all 14 of us in the pool, and my brothers and sisters and I often reminisce. Any mention of the Hollywood Pool always brings a smile to their faces and to mine. For all of us, being there and at the camp site are our favourite memories of childhood.

It was an adventure from the minute we got in the car: the journey there, making it to the bottom of the hill safely, climbing across the rocks without falling or burning our feet or getting nipped by crabs, finding shells, trying to catch fish, waves spilling over the top of us and sweeping us across the pool, and eventually arriving back at the camp site five or six hours later. It was so far removed from what we were normally doing in suburban Adelaide – going to our convent school, church on Sundays and visiting our grandparents on the weekend. At the Hollywood Pool we were out in the fresh air on the edge of the earth, away from everybody else in an extraordinary, pristine place.

As I get older I am determined to stay fit and strong so that I can keep making the trek along the cliff, down the soft sand and over the rocks to the Hollywood Pool for many more years to come.

Building
pools

DAVID BARTLETT

Endless games in the backyard

Fostered by the Bartlett family when he was 40 days old, David Bartlett spent his first five years living in the Hobart suburb of Moonah. In 1973, the Bartletts moved to Mount Nelson, high above Tasmania's capital city. The family of six children settled into life at their new house among the bush and on hot days cooled off at Hobart's Kingston Beach. In 1980, just before David turned 12, an important announcement was made that would have a big impact on his young life: the Bartlett family were putting in a pool!

I remember very clearly the day my father laid out plans on the kitchen table and announced to the family that we were getting a pool. After that it seemed to take an inordinate amount of time to build. It was seven or so years since our rambling six-bedroom AV Jennings house had been completed, but the backyard was still full of massive boulders that had been unearthed during the building process.

When work started on the pool, those boulders had to go, so large excavating equipment was brought in to the back of the block, which butted up against the bush. In one of the many photos my father took during the construction phase, there's a guy on a big earthmover, and as he enlarges the hole he's still digging up rocks. Eventually those boulders and rocks were moved to the edge of the bush, the hole was dug, foundations laid, the concrete poured, the tiles and pavers installed and the pool was completed. Finally we could start filling it with water from the garden hose, which ended up taking three days. My sister Catherine and I didn't wait for the chlorine to be added or for my father's intricate heating system to get to work. We were in straight away.

The pool was 11 metres long and about five or six metres wide. It was a standard rectangular shape with a slight curve on one side and a little triangle cut out in a corner where there were steps leading into the water. The interior was white concrete with a single row of ugly brown tiles around the top. They were probably the cheapest tiles they could find – by no stretch of the imagination were my parents rich; they were bringing up six children on a teacher's income. My father also tried to save money by installing the pavers around the pool himself. His expertise was maths teaching, not paving, so over a couple of years they sank to varying levels around the pool, and we were always stubbing our toes. The measure of a good summer for me was how many stubbed toes I had.

When it was completed our pool was the opposite of that image of a sparkling turquoise pool at a middle-class family home with a nice glass fence and manicured lawns around it. It was this pool with undulating, falling-apart pavers facing on to bushland and overhanging eucalypts that used to drop their leaves in the water, staining the bottom. Those leaves were the bane of my father's life and still are today. On the side of the pool closest to the bush there was a drop of about eight feet, so a fence was installed as soon as the pool was finished so that people didn't fall off the edge.

The other key part of the pool was the blue cover, which was also the bane of our existence. It wasn't like the fancy ones you see today that get rolled out. It was like blue bubble wrap that floated over the top of the pool. If you didn't put it on properly, my father got cross because of the leaves. He is more than 80 now but those eucalypts still drop a ton of leaves and drive him insane.

The eldest child in our family was a boy, then there were three girls, then me and the baby, another boy. They all had red hair and freckles and I had dark hair and dark skin. When the whole family and some friends used the pool, there'd be 20 people in and around it. There was only one other backyard pool in Mount Nelson, so we'd get kids knocking on our door to see if they could have a swim. My parents would always welcome them in, so at times there would be a crowd in the pool, but that wasn't the norm. Usually it would be my next-door neighbour

Owain and me in there until we were wrinkled or called to dinner.

In the 1970s and 80s there weren't a lot of houses in Mount Nelson, but we had houses on either side of us and Owain, my best friend on the planet, lived in one of them. He was a year or so older than me and his kitchen window looked into the side of our house. We had all sorts of secret signals that were invitations to either play cricket, roam the bush or swim in the pool. I even had one to tell Owain the water temperature, which didn't bother me as I swam in the pool all year round. I loved the cold water and the feeling of being completely invigorated afterwards. For everyone else, when the water hit 18 degrees, that's when the swimming season started. Others preferred the pool when Dad's home-made solar heating system was working properly and the water could be as warm as 27 degrees.

The pool was a place of invention for Owain and me and we spent thousands of hours playing in and around it. Owain held the record for swimming four and a half laps underwater, whereas I could only make four. Both of us nearly drowned trying to beat the record but we didn't think about that at the time. At the end of each day our fingers would be shrivelled and we'd have worn out the pads on our toes from running around the bottom of the pool on that old concrete surface that was slightly rough, like fine-grained sandpaper, and would tear your feet apart.

The deep end was about seven feet, so we'd make up all kinds of games involving diving for sinking bricks and

rings. We played pool volleyball, tennis, golf, cricket, basketball and had elaborate bomb-dive competitions. For
those we made our own scorecards to hold up for each
other like they do in real diving competitions. We'd get
points according to the degree of difficulty of the bomb,
such as adding a somersault, and we'd give them all elaborate names.

We had intricate sets of rules and regulations for each
of these games and we were always arguing over whether
one of us had broken a rule. With pool basketball you had
to bounce the ball on the surface of the water while you
were swimming; with pool tennis the rule was you had
three seconds to get to the ball and hit it back. There were
always challenges over whether one of us was counting
too fast.

Major discussions over rule compliance were part of
the fun and we never took it too far, not like schoolyard
cricket, when all of us would be very serious and there'd
be lots of disputes about whether someone was out or
not. Once we got back to the pool after those contentious
cricket games, it didn't matter if you'd had barneys all
day, because you returned to fun at the pool. The pool
was always the salvation and the place of forgiveness.

In those early years of high school, when I was going
through an angry period about my identity and feeling
different to everyone else because I was fostered, the pool
helped me in lots of ways. Before we got the pool, I was
an okay swimmer, but because of it I became quite a good
swimmer. I wasn't a great swimmer by any stretch of the

imagination but I was faster than anyone else in Year 10 at Taroona High except a girl my age called Anna, who is still a friend today. She was a really outstanding swimmer and had the potential to go much further than the school swimming carnival and inter-school events. I didn't like the constraints of school much but I did enjoy my involvement in swimming and in Year 10 I was the swimming captain. I was always the slowest runner because I was born with a problem with my foot and had eight surgeries before I was seven to try and fix it. So I enjoyed doing well at swimming at school.

High school was about forming new circles of friends, especially girls. Having one of only two back-yard pools in the neighbourhood from Grade 7 to Grade 10 was a pretty cool way of having friends around, and sometimes that encouraged the girls to come to my house. My parents had a lot of rules about girls coming over and they didn't like them being with me and my mates without supervision. They were very strict Christians and I think my father's reason for putting in the pool in the first place was so that my three older sisters would bring their boyfriends home rather than going out with them. I certainly had a lot of friends over and when they turned up at the house they didn't knock on the front door, they'd just walk down the side of the house to the pool area, where there was a rumpus room with a table tennis table and a cheap pool table. We'd spend all afternoon alternating between playing table tennis and pool and jumping in the water.

At some stage in my teenage years my parents built a shack down the coast. I didn't like going there as I thought it was boring, so sometimes I'd get to stay home and that's when I'd invite friends around to the pool, usually at night. At that time you could get a bottle of Stone's green ginger wine for $5.99 at the local bottle-o. My mates and I would invite the girls around and we'd sit around the pool drinking wine together and feeling pretty free. Most of us had our first sexual experiences in and around that pool. Nothing serious but lots of pashing off.

Our backyard pool in Mount Nelson gave me a space of my own because the rest of the family didn't use it as much as me. The idea that my older sisters would bring boyfriends home didn't happen. Most of the time it was my place and during those high school years when I was having issues about my identity, the pool was a refuge for me. It was also a place of great freedom, joy and friend-ship, especially with Owain, who after all these years is still my best mate, and jokes with me now that the only reason he was my friend was because I had a pool!

KIM METTAM

Plunging into beauty in Perth

When Kim Mettam's grandfather Frank arrived back in Western Australia after World War I, he was advised to swim in salt water to help heal his leg, which had been badly injured at the Battle of the Somme in 1916. He followed that advice and in 1930 bought a block of land at Perth's Trigg Beach, where he built a one-room weekender. Soon after, he started his life-long project of turning an extensive limestone reef into a protected swimming and snorkelling spot, which became known as Mettam's Pool. In the 1960s Kim often helped his grandfather remove 'one more rock' in his quest to perfect the pool.

As a child I was very close to my grandfather and I'd often stay over at his house just up the road from Mettam's Pool. I have vivid memories of looking up at the kitchen ceiling, which was made out of flattened kerosene tins, and noticing how the room in the middle had outside windows because the house was originally only one room. In the 1930s and 40s my grandparents and their three sons lived in the Perth suburb of Mount Lawley during the week and came out to the beach house on Friday nights. When Grandfather retired they moved there permanently. It was a magnificent spot with 180-degree views of the ocean.

We'd often retreat up to the beach house after several hours at Mettam's Pool, but we were never allowed in the house unless we had removed all the sand from ourselves under the outside shower. There was no gentle pressure on that shower – just a forceful cold blast! Grandfather used to get us to play soldiers and stand to attention while he checked if all the sand was washed off. He made my father and uncles do the same thing when they were boys. 'Suck in your tummy and puff out your chest,' he'd say. He'd show us how to do it but one time he miscalculated how much bigger his belly had become over the years and when he sucked in his stomach his pants fell down. My brother Brad and I burst out laughing. Grandfather was a lovely man, very laid back and not strict. He had this huge hole in his knee and he used to say to all his grand-children, 'Can you see the little mouse that lives in the hole in my knee?' and we would look and look, strug-gling to see the elusive mouse.

Before Grandfather came along, the area that is now Mettam's Pool was an extensive limestone reef just north of Trigg Island Beach and the famous Blue Hole, a natural suction force caused by treacherous underwater reefs. When I was a child I'd listen spellbound as my grandfather spoke about the dangers of the Blue Hole and how the current was like a giant invisible hand that reached up and dragged people under, trapping them beneath the reef. He'd talk about the people who had drowned there, including two brothers, a nun, and a brave rescuer who had plunged into the maelstrom and lost his own life while endeavouring to save another, and stories of how Grandfather himself had participated in searches for the bodies.

The beach Grandfather turned into Mettam's Pool wasn't as dangerous as the Blue Hole but it was pretty much unswimmable with the limestone reef virtually covering the whole area right to the shoreline. Grandfather's vision was to create a natural swimming pool by reshaping the reef. His hope was that the reef walls would become natural homes for sea creatures – but not white pointer sharks, which were just as threatening to West Australians as the Blue Hole. He also wanted to allow people a good lengthy stretch of water to swim in, so the reef needed to be cleared sufficiently to create this space. His other aim was to enable a soft sandy beach you could walk on, rather than hazardous hard rock.

To create the pool, he needed explosives. The limestone calcarenite rock was extremely hard. In the 1930s, explosives were difficult to come by, but it just so happened that at the same time my grandfather was planning the pool, the road behind it, the West Coast Highway, was being constructed. The road crew were blowing up bits of limestone to build the road, so for the price of a dozen cold bottles of beer my grandfather obtained the explosives. In order to create the holes to put the explosives in, my father and uncles and their cousins used to hold on to a giant crowbar and my grandfather would swing a sledge hammer and it would make a little chink in the reef and then he would turn the crowbar around a bit and then do it again. Slowly but surely, the crowbar would make a hole in the reef and when he'd gone down far enough he'd put the explosives in and blow out sections of the reef. The crowbar was an old axle salvaged from a horse and buggy rig.

I grew up with that crowbar – well, those crowbars. He actually had three – a big one, a medium one and a small one. My youngest brother, Todd, is the keeper of the large crowbar now and it hangs proudly on one of his walls. When I was a boy, I could barely hold it, it was very heavy. There was always one more rock my grandfather wanted to move and he'd ask his grandchildren to help him. He had a plan in his mind of what he was going to do and he'd brief whichever grandchild or grandchildren were assisting over that couple of weeks. At other times he'd clear sharp reef rocks from the beach so people could walk more easily along the sand. We all loved moving those rocks with him. It was definitely a labour of love.

One day when my middle brother Brad (who became a marine biologist) was helping in the pool, my grandfather pointed to a grey-haired man who was towelling himself dry on the beach and said, 'See that man, you should go up to him and say thank you.' Brad asked him why and he said, 'He is the man who brought me to safety when I was wounded on the battlefield in France. Without him, you would not have been born.' So Brad went up to the man, whose name was Fred Lampard, and told him what Grandfather had said, and he said, 'You're welcome.'

In the 1950s, members of the local community started helping Grandfather and a team of people joined him planting vegetation and stabilising the bank above the beach, which kept eroding and dumping dark soil on the sand. Coming back from the pool one day I got incinerated on that bank. It was a really hot day and I jumped out of the water and started sprinting up the hill and climbing up the bank of dark soil and very quickly the cooling effect of the water started to dissipate. Half-way up I felt like I was walking on hot coals and thought, 'What have I got myself into?' But there was nothing I could do but just keep going. When I got home my feet and hands were burnt from grabbing the soil of the bank to get up as quickly as possible. I got into trouble from my grandmother, who said it was a foolish thing to do.

Growing up in Perth in the 1960s, the summers were endless hot days. The relief came from the pool. I didn't know what air conditioning was, but the pool was far superior and what's more you could play and I'd make new friends every time I went there. At Mettam's Pool I discovered the joy of putting my head under water and realising a completely different world existed. When I learned to use flippers, a snorkel and face mask, everything looked so much bigger and more colourful under the water. Once you put the face mask on, a fairyland of wonderful sights opened up and everything seemed magnified and amplified. There were dazzling contrasting colours among the different marine life – the vivid colours of the coral and schools of swordfish, garfish and mullet, though I avoided the blowfish as they weren't very attractive. There were octopus, too, which were well camouflaged, but if you looked closely you could find them. When you went deeper into the pool there were darker parts with seaweed that for a young boy were a bit scary, so when I was small I stayed away from those.

In 1960, when I was seven, my mother took me down each morning to do the Western Australian Education Department swimming program, and my aim was to swim freestyle like Johnny Weissmuller in the 1930s Tarzan movies I watched at the local Saturday afternoon pictures. I'm not sure if I achieved the same look but I remember doing the strokes and learning to kick and dive between the teacher's legs. It was the first time I'd dived between the legs of an adult. After those lessons, I took refuge from the sun under Mum's beach umbrella. It had a very distinctive pattern of light purple, cream and red-orange that I could always spot among the maze of colourful umbrellas on the beach.

My mother was a real beauty. Her name was Valma, but she was known as Val and in her younger days she'd won beauty competitions in the south-west of the state. At Mettam's she'd sunbake and socialise with everyone while still keeping an eye on us kids, and she always had a cold drink and honey sandwiches for us. It took real skill to keep the sand out of the sandwich, which after a few hours developed a crystallised taste because the heat would make the honey go sugary. Any new friends I made, I'd bring them back to our spot and they'd have a sandwich and a drink too.

Mum mainly came to the pool when I was small as Dad did shift work in his role as a proofreader at the *West Australian* newspaper. But Dad was the one who taught me to float at Mettam's Pool, which gave me the confidence to learn to swim. He explained what was going to happen and then he took his hands away. I floated successfully first time and I remember the incredible feeling of drifting as your body took over and kept you from sinking. I was seven and it was a wonderful new sensation. Although Mettam's Pool was very calm, there'd be these gentle ripples of water and that rocking while you were floating was lovely.

I often explored the marine life in and around the edges of the pool, and one day I decided I was going to count how many crabs I could see. I think I got up to 80 or nearly 100. As a small boy I was fascinated by how they lived and their little houses in the rocks. When my cousins also stayed at my grandparents' house, our grandmother used to get us to go down and collect periwinkles, which were a cross between a mussel and a snail.

There were lots of them around the limestone reef, and after we'd collected them, she'd cook them up. Some of my cousins liked them but they were not very appetising to me. There were abalone in the pool too, but we used not to bother with them. They were left alone and grew really big. In fact, they were downright annoying because they'd get barnacles on the outside of their shells and these could cut your feet. Today abalone is prized and much rarer, and there's only a few hours each year when people are allowed to take them from the pool.

The little caves around the beach made for fantastic escapades and as a boy I would wonder whether I'd discover a smuggler's ring or spies in hiding. My favourite pastime was playing pirates in the caves on the shoreline, imagining I'd find a buried treasure of gold Spanish doubloons. I figured I could bring prosperity to the family if I found a chest full of gold and buy Dad a new car and get Mum a new house. That was my theory. I was also on a quest to find a natural pearl in the pool and would spend hours in the water searching. Sometimes I'd draw pictures of the shells I found in the pool and on the beach, and I became quite an expert at building sandcastles. One year I came second in a sandcastle-building competition at Mettam's when I made a ship with various different levels.

Occasionally I joined my female cousins – Paula, Lorraine and Glenys – on expeditions in the evening exploring what was left of the sandhills above Mettam's Pool. They were a few years older than me and were always talking about boys and I'd be thinking how I'd much prefer to find some friends to play pirates. But one day when I was about 12, I met a very pretty girl at the pool and we had a wonderful day frolicking in the water. We had so much fun and at the end of the day she said can we meet tomorrow. And I said yes. Tomorrow came but for some reason my grandparents wouldn't let me go to the pool. About four years later when I was at a friend's party I came across that girl again and she told me she'd waited all day for me. It was a fantastic day and it was probably when I realised how beautiful girls were, particularly in bathers.

I kept swimming regularly at Mettam's Pool through my teenage years and when I got into surfing I used to store my surfboard under my grandparents' beach house. We'd spend the day surfing at Triggs and swim at Mettam's Pool and then come up to my grandfather's for a drink and to put the surfboards away. He loved that and he used to think I had some lovely girlfriends.

Grandfather's life's work was to create a pool that was part of the natural landscape. Today you wouldn't know that it was man-made. Mettam's Pool was an anchor point of pride in my family and it has had an impact on my outlook in life and my belief that if you work hard enough and smart enough you can achieve anything. The fact that the pool carried my grandfather's name gave me a sense of identity and it contributed to my confidence. It has also meant that I always wanted to honour my name and follow what my grandfather said, 'Do the right thing, the honourable thing and recognise and praise people for their achievements.' He also used to say, 'If you don't have a good word to say about someone, then don't say anything.'

After having such a terrible experience in the war, he liked the serenity of being beside the sea. He often used to talk about the huge contrast between the sounds of violence and death on the battlefield and the peaceful sound of the waves breaking on Triggs and North Beach. He called it a lifelong tonic.

I also love the sound of the ocean and I'll always have fond memories of falling asleep in my grandparents' house after one of many wonderful days at Mettam's Pool. All snug and comfortable under the blankets with the smell of the fresh sea breeze blowing through the open window, I'd listen to the ocean waves falling softly onto the beach until I was asleep. The next morning I'd wake up and be ready to start another day's adventure at Mettam's Pool, hopeful of finding that special pearl, buried treasure or a pretty girl.

LILY SISA

Dreaming big in Lightning Ridge

In the mid-1980s, when Lily Sisa was in primary school in the opal-mining town of Lightning Ridge in outback New South Wales, the only options for cooling off in summer were the local dams. There was no river in the town and the hot bore baths didn't cut it when the temperature often soared into the 40s. The closest pool was an hour's drive away at Walgett, so in 1988, when Lily was 12, she and her younger sister and three friends launched a 'Pool for Lightning Ridge' fundraising campaign.

Our dream to get a pool in Lightning Ridge started when my younger sister Simone, our friends Kelly and Crystal Mahoney and Tammy Jakitsch and I were doing swimming training three afternoons a week at the Walgett pool. Walgett is about an hour's drive from Lightning Ridge and Dad and some of the other parents would drive us there. On those trips back and forth we used to talk about how it was so hot and we wished we had our own pool in Lightning Ridge. We whinged for a couple of years and then in 1988 the five of us decided to try and raise the money ourselves.

Kelly and I had just started high school in Walgett and the three other girls were still in primary school in Lightning Ridge. We were all still doing swimming training at Walgett pool, and on those journeys back to Lightning Ridge we'd talk about what we were going to do. For the past 20 or so years, a group of adults in town had been fundraising to get a pool, but over that time they'd only raised $33000, which wasn't enough to build an Olympic-size pool. They'd also tried to get government funding, but had never been successful because we were considered too small – in 1988, Lightning Ridge had an official population of less than 2000 people. There were probably another 500 people camped out at the opal mines who weren't registered on the electoral roll and there were always people in town who didn't want to be officially known, but even if they'd been counted, we would probably still be too small.

When we set up our committee of five girls aged between nine and 12, we didn't really have much idea of how much we had to raise. Someone mentioned needing at least $450000, which seemed an enormous amount, but we didn't think too much about that. We decided just to have a go. One of the first things we did was open a bank account, and when the old pool fundraising committee was disbanded, they deposited the $33000 they had raised into our account. At our first meeting we allocated all the various committee positions. Our friend Kelly, who lived across the road from us, was the president, my younger sister Simone and I were the vice presidents, Kelly's younger sister Crystal was the treasurer and their cousin, our friend Tammy, was the secretary. Around the same time an adult committee of 15 parents was also set up to support us. Our mum and dad, Trudy and Richard Mallouk, were on that committee and Sharon Mahoney, Kelly and Crystal's mum, was too.

Mum and Dad were encouraging right from the start. Dad is originally from France and Mum is from Germany and they came to Lightning Ridge with one suitcase between them in 1969. They made a bit of money from opal mining and stayed. Like most people in the town they were not into red tape and if they wanted to make something happen they just got on and did it themselves, so they were very enthusiastic about our committee and encouraged us.

The first thing we did was to have a cake stall in the main street, and every fortnight we helped Mum make 60 cakes. She's a great cook, and each week she'd produce these beautiful German apple cakes and marble, banana and carrot cakes and these expensive ones with cream and cherries on top which we sold for $5 each. We'd help her with the mixing and chopping up and, of course, eating the leftover cake mix. On Saturdays we'd set up the cakes on big trestle tables in the main street in front of the butcher's shop. We'd also load up cakes into a freezer basket and walk around to the businesses and sell to the people who couldn't get out of their shops. A few people would say they didn't want to buy a cake but most people in the town got used to us being there on Saturdays and they'd turn up to buy one of Mum's delicious creations. It was exciting when we counted up the money we'd made at our monthly meetings. We also recorded the minutes and talked about what we were going to do next.

Another fundraising idea we came up with was asking people to buy a tile for $5 and we'd put the donor's name on an honour board at the pool when it was completed. We had a temporary board made up which we displayed outside the courthouse showing how many tiles had been sold. Some people just bought one tile but others, including the local service station, sponsored lanes for $15 000. With the support of the adult committee, other fundraising events were held, like discos and a country music festival, and each week meat trays were raffled at the pub.

Dad was always encouraging local businesses and opal miners to donate to the pool fund and he also lent the committee the money to buy cars for art union raffles. He wasn't scared to ask people for donations and he used to say, 'You won't know if you don't ask.' We were all very happy when a Sydney opal dealer donated a sapphire ring, and when a local artist donated some paintings to raffle. On those hot days when we'd walk around town selling raffle tickets we'd wish we didn't have to do it, but the thought of not suffering any more hot summers kept us going. We were very dedicated, and the people in the town could see the amount of money coming from the tiles and all the fundraising activities as they saw the latest tally in the local paper. Gradually they realised they had to take us seriously.

We didn't wait to have the total amount of money we needed to build the pool. As it came in, work started with Dad as supervisor. He and other members of the adult committee got the support of tradespeople in town who volunteered their services for free. We had to pay for the materials – the cement, fencing and other supplies – but the town's electricians and plumbers and work-for-the-dole guys provided free labour and Gary Stone, a local opal miner who had a lot of big machinery, dug the hole for the pool free of charge.

When the *Sydney Morning Herald* did a story on us five girls, which was followed up on *A Current Affair* and on ABC Radio, we started to get donations from all around Australia. We got messages of support from people in cities and country towns. A few people donated $100 but most were small amounts like $10 – every bit helped and it was great to have the support of individuals and communities around the country. We also quite enjoyed doing the media interviews, which we thought were very exciting.

The other thing that helped our fundraising was that in early 1990 we won a number of awards, including the *Sydney Morning Herald* Youth Award, a Channel Ten Young Achievers' Award, and an Australia Day Committee National Community Event of the Year award.

Prime Minister Bob Hawke was at the ceremony to present us with the Australia Day award and we came up with the idea of getting the youngest member on our committee, Crystal Mahoney, to make a short speech asking him for help.

We didn't hear anything more for a couple of weeks or so and then a letter arrived saying the federal government would contribute $140 000 towards the pool. Funding support also came from the NSW Department of Sport and Recreation, Telecom, as it was called back then, Walgett Shire Council, and the Prime Club gave us $20 000 to ensure it was disability-friendly. As 1990 progressed we were getting closer to our target and we were more and more confident we could complete the pool before Christmas that year. Dad contacted Dawn Fraser and asked her if she would officially open the pool. When she said yes, a date was set for the opening on 5 December 1990. He also rang Leo Schofield, who we had spoken to earlier in the campaign on his ABC radio program and for his column in the *Sydney Morning Herald*, and he passed on an invitation to the opening to everyone around Australia who had contributed.

It was 45 degrees on the official opening day and there were so many people gathered at the pool. All the opal miners left their mines for the day and came in and everyone who lived in town was there, plus visitors from other parts of the north-west – Tamworth and nearby places like St George in south-west Queensland. The five of us were very excited and when we dived in to do the first lap with Dawn Fraser what I remember most is that the water wasn't clear – it was a milky colour.

It was all a bit of a rush to get the 50-metre pool and small wading pool to a stage that it could be opened and they'd run out of time to get the chlorination right. But that didn't stop anybody from getting in the pool because after we'd finished our inaugural lap, everyone jumped in, many fully clothed. A plaque was erected acknowledging that it was opened by Dawn Fraser, and a local man, Peter Rosso, made a huge sign out of tiny stones with an image of a mine shaft in the middle and the words 'Five Star Lightning Ridge Olympic Pool', which was to recognise us five girls. It was a great day and we were proud of what we did, but we didn't make a big fuss because really it was a whole community effort from all the people of Lightning Ridge.

In those first few weeks the pool was open, I had to pinch myself on those really hot days and I remember thinking, *Oh my God, we can actually go to the pool*. It was such a relief not to have to get on a bus or wait to be driven for an hour to go to the Walgett pool. Now all the young people in town had somewhere to go and all our friends would hang out there with our coconut oil on. It was also lovely to be able to exercise and do laps as it was hard to walk or run in the heat with all the flies. In those early days the pool used to stay open till 9 p.m. and it was fantastic swimming there on those hot nights.

The opening of the pool wasn't the end of our work, as right from the start Mum got Simone and me to help her out in the canteen, which she volunteered to run. The pool has never been a council pool, it's always been run by the Lightning Ridge Olympic Pool Association, which was mainly made up of the members of the adult fundraising committee, including Mum and Dad. A pool manager was employed, but everyone else was a volunteer, and all the money made on the entry fee and in the canteen went back into the pool and into the next project – first a sports centre, and then a theme park pool.

There was no way the association could afford to buy all the features for the theme park pool, but the members knew a man in town called Lightning Les, who made things out of foam and steel. He made all the features, like an open-mouthed frog – the kids could slide down the frog's tongue – and a mushroom that became a waterfall, octopus, swans, turtles and seals, and a local artist, Russell Klein, painted them. The whole town was excited again when the theme park pool, right next to the Olympic pool, opened in January 1998. It was incredible fun being on the slides, in the rapid river pool and the wave pool.

Some people may have thought that we had enough pools in Lightning Ridge, but Dad had a plan to build an indoor diving pool based on the one at Homebush that had been built for the 2000 Sydney Olympic Games. By now he was very experienced at overseeing pool projects, so he also supervised the construction of the diving pool. When it was nearly finished in 2011, he didn't want all the walls to be bare concrete, so he encouraged my sister

Simone, who is very creative, to paint some murals on the walls.

She did a brilliant job painting a massive pirate ship, sunken treasure, fish, starfish, shells, a scuba diver, sharks and a beach scene. She also created a sort of hall of fame of the main people who were involved in making all the different pools possible. She painted us five girls as mermaids, and put all our names on little shell clips. Dad is there as Where's Wally in red and white swimmers, and Gary Stone, the opal miner who provided all the machinery and dug the holes for all three pools at no charge, is honoured in a sign washed up on the sand saying 'Stoney's Pool Building Service'. Ian Woodcock, a former mayor who played a major role in the building of the pools, is pictured walking his dog. Some of the long-time committee members are also featured, including the local plumber, Ged Hutchinson, who Simone painted fixing something underwater with his goggles on.

In the years since that diving pool has been opened we've hosted some high-level events, including the School Sports Australia Diving Championships; the US junior diving team has trained here and we've produced a number of state diving champions. All the pools are not only somewhere for the young people of the town to go but they are a tourist attraction and bring groups to Lighting Ridge, especially from places nearby, which is good for the local economy.

Since the late 1980s I have been connected to the pools in one way or other, and since 2012 I have been the president of the Lightning Ridge Olympic Pool Association, taking over from my dad, who turned 81 in 2019. My mother is 74 now and only recently stepped down from running the canteen, but she's still the association's treasurer. From 2003 till 2015, my husband Roman was the manager of the pool, and since they were little, our two boys have swum at the pool. They are 10 and seven now and don't know Lightning Ridge without the pools. They are both in the Piranhas Swimming Club and the diving club and my older son can't wait to be big enough to become a lifeguard.

The council provides a subsidy to partially run the complex, but we are still fundraising through the entry fee and the canteen so that we can pay for the maintenance of the pools. My role as president is a volunteer position and we continue to rely on our volunteers – if anyone can do anything for free, it really helps. We still have the board up at the pool with all the names of people who bought tiles, and another one acknowledging people who donated money or items for raffles. Recently we replaced the glass panel and local artist John Murray refreshed his painting on the wave pool wall for free, which is typical of people in this town.

When I look back to that time between 1988 and 1990 when we were working hard to get a pool for Lightning Ridge, it was five girls who started it but it was the amazing Lightning Ridge community that built it in the end. The people here have beautiful hearts and community spirit. There are more than 50 different nationalities at the local school and a strong Indigenous community and everyone is accepted here. Lightning Ridge is unique with the landscape and the mining and the variety of people who live here. And if people can help they will. During those two years, we learned about how much hard work was involved in building a pool, about the kindness and generosity of people, and how anything is possible if you believe in something and work hard enough to achieve it.

MERV KNOWLES

A bonzer brother
at Manuka

When architect Walter Burley Griffin designed
Canberra, he envisaged a swimming baths for
Australia's new capital city, but when five-year-old
Merv Knowles moved there in 1928, there was no
pool. His water-loving father wasn't happy with the
limited options for cooling off in the bush capital's
hot summers and joined with other public servants
to campaign for a proper pool. Three years later,
when the swimming pool at Manuka was officially
opened, eight-year-old Merv was one of the first to
dive in.

When we arrived in Canberra from Melbourne in
1928, the only swimming we had was two swimming holes on the Molonglo River, one near the Kingston Powerhouse and one at Acton. Dr Cumpston, who
was the Director-General of Health and lived near us at
Forrest, had the water tested at the Powerhouse and said,

'My kids are not going to swim in that.' So, he and Dad (Sir George Knowles, who in 1932 became head of the Attorney-General's Department) decided to get organised to get a pool.

They wanted a 55-yard pool and in the original plans it was, but when the Depression got in the way the government wanted to reduce the size. Dr Cumpston, Dad and other public servants involved in the pool campaign got into a bargaining situation with the government but it didn't do them any good. They decided on 33 and a third yards – 100 feet in length and 40 feet wide – and we ended up with six lanes instead of eight.

It was officially opened on 26 January 1931, but my sister Jean and brothers George and Lindsay and me, and the Cumpston kids, were allowed in for a swim a couple of weeks before it opened. There was only one dressing shed completed then – the boys' one – so they let the boys in the two families swim in the morning and the girls in the afternoon.

At the official opening we all gathered just outside the pool. There was nothing around it, no lawn, no fence, just a paddock, so the pool entrance looked rather grand in that stark environment, like a much smaller version of Parliament House, completed four years earlier. The words 'THE SWIMMING POOL' were inscribed in block letters across the top of the cream-coloured brick building, and on either side of the glass doors were columns like smaller versions of something you'd see in ancient Rome.

I was eight and I remember it as a great day as we finally had somewhere good to swim. Arthur Blakeney, who was Minister for Home Affairs and lived on Mugga Way, not far from us, performed the opening and then we were all allowed to swim. The pool was set up in a way that you went in through the entrance into the boys' or girls' change rooms, and before you entered the pool area you walked through a footbath with a shower over the top. You couldn't come into the pool any other way, so fair enough, we were all washed before we got in.

We had all the Causeway kids at the pool and they weren't always bathed. The Causeway was down behind the railway station at Kingston where all the working-men's places were. They worked in the printing office, the Powerhouse and around the Kingston shops and like us their kids all went to Telopea Park School just near the pool. There was only one school then and some of the kids from the Causeway used to come to school without shoes.

When the pool opened at the beginning of October each season, there was a tradition to be the first in the water. It involved a lot of push and shove and jostling and when Scotty or Davis, whoever was running the place at the time, flung the doors open, there'd be a rush and we'd race in to see who could hit the water first. I usually got beaten by my big brother Lindsay, who was faster than me, but I still made it first about four times. It was always a fun game.

In those early days of Canberra, everyone was looking for something to do outside work and school hours and on weekends. The pool was the social centre where the young people met to swim, sunbake, dive and socialise. There's a book about the pool called *That's Where I Met My Wife: A story of the first swimming pool in the national capital at Canberra*, and I think a lot of that happened in those days. It was definitely the place to be in summer and sometimes they'd have to close the doors for a while when they couldn't fit in any more people.

I used to swim in the morning, first thing before we had breakfast, and then sometimes at lunch and then back again in the afternoons after school. There would be 200 kids there after school. We all had lockers so we could leave our gear there. In the 1930s and 40s there were rules on the types of swimming togs you could wear at the pool. Men and boys couldn't go topless – you couldn't just have trunks. I had a set of trunks with a belt and a zipper and I could put the top on with the zipper if I was swimming at Manuka; if I went down the coast to Narooma where we had a house, I zipped off the top.

I always loved swimming – you're weightless, it's relaxing and I enjoyed seeing how fast I could get to the deep end. My brother Lindsay held the record for swimming the length in under 16 seconds. I could never get under 17 seconds. I always swam in lane one or two; they were considered the boys' lanes as they were on the side of the pool where the men's change rooms and sunbaking area were. The two sunbaking areas were totally enclosed and while I didn't spend too much time in them, I'm suffering today because of the sun.

We also had a diving tower, which they pulled down because of the insurance risk, but I wasn't much of a diver. I left that to Owen 'Crusty' Taverner, who was also a champion swimmer and later managed the pool, followed by his son 'Tav'. We had a good range of divers at the pool in the 1930s and 40s, including Bobby Baker. He was from the north side of Canberra, which early on was a big distinction. There was Ainslie, Braddon and Reid on the north side and Barton, Manuka, Kingston, Griffith, Red Hill and Forrest on the south side.

We all belonged to the swimming club – my two brothers, my sister and me – and for a period Dad was the president of the club and later patron. We had Wednesday night carnivals and a full range of championships and water polo. During the time when my brother Lindsay and Bill Dullard were vying with each other, it would be nothing to have 300, 400 people for the Wednesday night carnival. Lindsay was a good swimmer. He was club champion and he became Sydney University champion and All Australian Universities Swimming Champion where he knocked 14 seconds off the 400 yards intervarsity record. I was expected to be as good, but I never was. I was club champion twice, in 1940 and 1941, but that was because the big boys like Lindsay were away at the war.

Lindsay was a bonzer older brother and a good bloke. He did an Arts degree at Sydney University and then said to Father that he wanted to fly. By the time World War II came around he was a fighter pilot. He was just 24 when he was killed in aerial combat with a German Messer-schmitt fighter over Libya in 1941. He was one of nine from the Manuka swimming club and water polo team who were killed in the war, including his swimming rival Bill Dullard. They are all remembered in a plaque at the pool that was hung in the foyer in 1947 and restored in 2018 thanks to the Friends of Manuka Pool and a grant from the Department of Veterans' Affairs.

I thought we did a lot of training but it was nothing compared to today. Three lengths were a hundred yards and a mile was 53 laps. But I left the mile swims to Lind-say, who used to say he could go as fast as he wanted. It was just a question of how much he trained, which they've all proved since. I had the embarrassing situation one year of winning the men's 400 yards and the girls were two seconds faster than me. I remember one classic 800-yard race I competed in. I started the evening by having a game of water polo, which was half an hour or more, and lo and behold I then had to do an 800-yard swim. Len Major was my rival. Lenny went to work for 2CS and had a career in radio, but he swam along with me till about 400 and then he disappeared. At the end of it I said, 'What happened to you?' and he said, 'I got tired.' I said, 'But you hadn't played water polo,' and he said, 'No, but I still got tired.' He just stopped so I won that race.

I loved water polo and was captain at one stage. We used to train at 5.30 in the evening when it was all peace and quiet. Just before the war this fellow came to the pool while seven or eight of us boys were throwing the ball

around. This fellow dived in and said, 'Give us a chuck.'
We threw him the ball and it came back like a rocket. So
we threw it to him again and it went somewhere else like
a rocket. We got talking to him and it turned out he was
George Molnar, the political cartoonist. His cartoons were
brilliant. Anyway, he said, 'You chaps shouldn't be in the
water,' and we said, 'Why not?' He said we should be in
the two sunbaking areas learning to catch the water polo
ball one-handed and throw it one-handed. So we did that
for a while and then we asked him if he'd like to be our
coach and he said yes. I believe he learnt to play water
polo in his home country, Hungary. He was exceptional.
He could get high out of the water up to the lower part of
his hips because he was so strong in the legs underwater.
He could also make the ball flip this way or that, and we
had him.

One weekend our club invited the Sydney Spit Club
down to Manuka Pool for a round of water polo matches.
Over the two days they played us, the Canberra team and
the Duntroon Cadets and Staff. The only game they lost
was to our team with George Molnar in the centre. A
water polo team is seven players and he was the centre
man. I was right wing. I would have been 17, I suppose.

I really loved water polo practice and working on
my ability to catch a ball with one hand and flick it one
way or another or back where it came from. We were not
allowed to use two hands, except the goalie. For a while
we had Tim Ingram as goalie, who did all the tiling of the
four steps in the corners of the pool. He was apprenticed

to his father Adam, who did the tiling of the whole pool. Tim was six feet two or three and had arms that stretched from one side of the goal to the other, a great asset for stopping goals. Sadly, his youngest brother Ian was one of the nine from the pool who were killed in World War II.

I managed to keep out of trouble most of the time when I was at the pool. The managers Scotty and Davis were pretty strict, and there were all sorts of signs around the pool saying what you could and couldn't do, including one that said, 'No spitting and running', so you could walk and spit! I was only little – under 10 stone – still am, but at one stage I had a support role as an honorary inspector, which involved being a bit of a policeman if people were doing the wrong thing.

Everybody who lived in Canberra in the 1930s, 40s and 50s went to the pool – all the kids and teenagers from the north and south sides, some of the parliamentarians, the public servants and the working men and their families – as it was the only place to swim until the Canberra Olympic Pool opened in 1955. I was there morning, noon and night during the season with all the water polo team and all my mad friends. It was home to me and I still love it today, nearly 90 years on from the opening day.

Historic
pools

ELLEN CONNOR

The campaign to save Fitzroy Pool

When Ellen Connor was growing up in inner-city Melbourne in the 1980s and 90s, a favourite place was the Fitzroy Pool – one of the city's earliest pools when it opened in 1908. Nearly 90 years later, in October 1994, the commissioners of the newly formed City of Yarra Council announced its closure. With her father, Danny Connor, a regular swimmer at the pool, 14-year-old Ellen became involved in the six-week campaign to save the much-loved facility, famous beyond Fitzroy for featuring in Helen Garner's 1977 novel *Monkey Grip*.

In the mid to late 1980s, when I was at Clifton Hill Primary School, I used to attend an after-school and vacation care program that wasn't far from the Fitzroy Pool. During the school holidays and on hot days after school we would get taken to the pool. I was about six or seven when I first went there and I always remember how those old turnstiles seemed massive in comparison to me, and I felt they were going to beat me up. I remember Carl, who was one of the people who looked after the pool. He had a moustache and he'd always greet us with a smile when he took our money and let us in.

The pool smelt like chlorine and the concrete under your feet. There was always a great vibe and it was a really friendly place. We'd swim in the smaller children's pool and the big 50-metre pool where they used to have a water-slide. It was one of those tall, twisty, standing ones and you'd line up and slide down it into the shallow end of the pool. We'd have so much fun for ages and we'd never want to leave when the carers said we had to go. We'd always be begging for just one more turn on the slide.

My parents split up when I was quite young so I spent half my time in Northcote and then Brunswick with Mum and the other half with Dad at his place in Collingwood which was near Fitzroy Pool. Fitzroy is very close to the city and when I was growing up it was a lively, bohemian place with a diverse population. It had old sandstone cottages and terraces and Atherton Gardens, one of the largest public housing complexes in Melbourne, and lots of kids from there came to the pool. In the late 1980s most of them were migrants and refugees from Asian countries, as well as a few Greeks and Italians. There was always a mixture of kids at the pool but we'd all play together. My favourite spot was near the kids' pool, where there was a beautiful shade area for us to lay our towels down. Our other spot was the grandstand area on the side of the pool facing Cecil Street, which was nice if you wanted a bit of sun. We used to move between the two.

I spent a lot of the summer holidays at Fitzroy Pool playing Marco Polo with my friends, and at the end of the day we'd go down to Brunswick Street and get an ice cream. It was a big part of my childhood, especially when I was at Dad's. I'd often leave him a note and say, 'I've gone down the pool,' or he'd leave me one saying he was there and to join him. When I was still in primary school and in the early years of high school, I had a little tradition of going to the pool with my friends on Christmas Eve, because over that period we'd all be doing family things and wouldn't see each other. It was our chance to say have a great Christmas and we'd exchange a gift, have a bit of a play and a swim and arrange to meet up over the summer holidays.

Dad did squad at 5 a.m. at the pool and at one stage he got me involved in an all-ages swimming group. He was very connected to the pool, and like everyone else he only found out that it was going to close when it was reported in *The Age* on 10 October 1994. No one had had any warning that it was going to be closed and there had been no consultation before the decision was made; supposedly it was losing money.

When Dad and a whole lot of other people heard the terrible news they quickly set up a committee and started the Save Fitzroy Pool campaign. Right from the start Dad was heavily involved, along with Leigh Hubbard, Clare Giddens, Dave Lane, Lorna Harding – so many people, from all different backgrounds. I was 14 and a half then and I also got involved in the campaign. I was one of the youngest campaigners and one of the first things I did was have a jelly bean guessing competition. It was just a little fundraiser that I thought of myself and I put all these jelly beans in a jar and I counted every one of them. I knew there were exactly 200 jelly beans in there and I had a sign on the jar saying: *Put a dollar in, have a guess and your dollar will go towards the Save Fitzroy Pool campaign.* It was on the counter at the front desk of the pool and I would go and check it frequently. I noticed the jelly beans were dwindling. Some of the campaigners were taking one when they felt like something sweet. I think they must have thought, *Oh, she's a kid, she won't know.* Dad was eating them, too, so I made him buy me some new jelly beans to top it up.

The first major thing the Save Fitzroy Pool group did was hold a rally at Brunswick Oval in Fitzroy North. More than 1500 people turned up, and many were really angry about the sudden closure of such a vital community place. Two days after that, on 21 October, we occupied the pool complex to stop it being bulldozed. For more than a month campaigners were at the pool, and a whole group of us slept on mattresses in the gym area.

One time we had a funny night when we were all trying to go to sleep. It was pretty late and we kept hearing these cars driving along Alexandra Parade beeping their horns. We were all wondering what was going on and none of us could get to sleep. And then we realised we'd left the sign up outside that said: *Toot to save Fitzroy Pool*. I remember my dad and a few other guys ran downstairs in their boxer shorts and took the sign down for the night so we could get some sleep.

I stayed overnight at the pool at least a couple of nights during the week and on weekends. I remember waking up and wondering where I was, then I'd remind myself I was at the pool. The gym had pretty thin walls, so you'd hear when people were going up and down the stairs or going off to the change rooms to have showers in the mornings. We were lucky enough to have sponsorship from a number of local cafés and businesses like the bakery in Fitzroy. Each week a delivery of bagels would come in, and other local eateries and cafés provided us with food throughout the campaign, or a restaurant would give us a voucher and invite us to have dinner there and share our story of the pool.

In the early 1990s, the pool was only open in summertime, and in winter it was emptied. During the period we occupied the pool, some of the kids and I used to play games of backyard cricket in the empty pool, and once we had a barbeque in there. It was such a surreal experience to be able to play cricket inside the pool and run up and down the length of it. We'd play music and dance in the pool, and from that developed the idea of seeing how many people would fit in Fitzroy Pool as a mass protest that would get media attention.

Before that happened, more than 2000 people marched down Brunswick Street to draw attention to the

Save Fitzroy Pool campaign. At that march, I was one of the kids up the front with the banner. That's when the comedian John Clarke came up and introduced himself. It was a really hot day and he bought me and some of the other kids an icy pole. He was a regular swimmer at Fitzroy Pool and really passionate about saving it.

He was a lovely man. Another time he came up to me after I'd played the clarinet at a rally. I'd composed a song made up of little riffs that reminded me of the pool and water and he said, 'That was good.' The cartoonist Kaz Cooke also supported the campaign and she designed our Save Fitzroy Pool poster. After that rally up Brunswick Street the 2000 marchers filled the empty pool. It was a massive crowd of people all standing in the pool, plus some on the grandstand.

We did so many things to get support for our campaign, including a candlelight vigil involving all the shops along Brunswick Street lighting a candle in their front window for an hour one night in support of Fitzroy Pool. A group of us went up to Brunswick Street that night and I carried this really huge lit candle as we walked along the street. In the Fringe Festival parade, which was centred around Fitzroy and Brunswick Street, we had a Friends of Fitzroy Pool float with everyone dressed in vintage swimming costumes. I played some music on my clarinet and all us kids had our Save Fitzroy Pool t-shirts on. We also had a benefit concert at the Royal Derby Hotel with all sorts of bands playing to raise awareness of what was going on at the pool.

One night we had another fundraiser at the Carlton movie house with the film *Monkey Grip*, which features Fitzroy Pool. Noni Hazelhurst was in it and there were lots of scenes at the pool and the famous *Aqua Profunda* sign. I learned that the sign was painted on the wall at the deep end in 1953 by the pool manager at the time, James Murphy, because he was constantly rescuing migrant children at that end of the pool. They later found out the word *Aqua* should have been spelt *Acqua*. At 14, I hadn't been aware of the book *Monkey Grip* but I was after the movie based on it was screened for the Save Fitzroy Pool campaign.

On 30 November, nearly six weeks after the pool had been closed, we got word that it would reopen by Christmas. I found out when my dad called me and said, 'I've got great news. *We've won. It's a victory.*' The first thing that had to be done was to fill the pool with water again. Dad asked me to bring some friends down after school to be in the pool as it was being filled up as the media were going to be there. A couple of big fire trucks came to fill the pool and it was amazing being in there as those big hoses poured water in.

In the middle of December we had a big party to celebrate being able to get back in the pool and enjoy our space. We had a sausage sizzle, fairy floss and slushies, and someone rowed a small boat across the pool to re-enact the official opening in October 1908. We also had bands like Tiddas playing. I remember being in awe of the three women in Tiddas. They became my role models and I became heavily influenced by their music after that gig. After their first set, Lou Bennett, one of the band members, ran off and jumped in the pool. There was a carnival atmosphere, with heaps of people who had come on rallies and to the benefits and marches. After that first year, we decided to keep it an annual celebration, so the next year we did another one, and because I was doing music at high school I got to organise the bands – Sarah Carroll, the Cajun Aces, Joe Geia and Carol Fraser. One of my science teachers was in Cajun Aces.

It was a really happy and positive feeling – we had saved Fitzroy Pool from closing. It was something that connected my dad and me – the campaign and the enjoyment of Fitzroy Pool. It was all done in the period before social media – no Facebook, Twitter or Instagram, so we'd do lots of runs to put up posters about rallies, marches and events and people wrote letters to the newspapers, put out statements and got stories in the media. There were a lot of people involved – even the deputy prime minister, Brian Howe, supported our campaign; his kids swam at the pool. It was grassroots action and we had huge support. There was a big sense of community among the people involved in the campaign.

Once it was open again it was fantastic. It was a hive of activity and we could all go there and reconnect with our friends. Back then you knew every second face at the pool and Fitzroy was a safe and caring community. It was a great honour to be involved in saving the pool at that young age and being able to help with something I was passionate about. It was a sense of achievement that I'd contributed to saving something and I felt good knowing that people could enjoy the place again.

Being involved in the Save Fitzroy Pool campaign definitely had an impact on my life, and my political attitude came out after that. Since moving to Geelong eight years ago I've run for Geelong City Council twice and I've joined the local Labor Party. I'm heavily involved in campaigning and supporting all my local Labor candidates when they are running for parliament and I'm also involved in the Change the Rules campaign for fair pay and fair work conditions. I can trace that involvement back to when I was campaigning to save Fitzroy Pool, a time when I learned a lot about how to be seen and heard.

DIANE VUKELIC

Toasting a Swan River icon

Diane Vukelic grew up in the coastal Western Australian town of Bunbury, two and a half hours south of Perth. From 1968, when she was six, until she was nearly 10, she and her older sister and younger brother spent a week each summer holidays learning to swim at Perth's Nedlands Baths, which had been built on the Swan River in 1909. Her teachers were her great-aunty and her grandmother, who migrated to Australia from Denmark and ran the baths from 1953 until they were closed in 1975.

Nedlands Baths were near the University of Western Australia and close to a pub called Steve's on the Swan River foreshore. Steve's was the place everyone went to when I was at university in the early 1980s. When we were all outside having a drink, I'd look across to the baths and say, 'My family used to live there.' Then everybody would tell me they had had lessons at the Pedersen

School of Swimming at the baths, and they'd talk about those strict white-haired women, my great-aunty and my grandmother, who pushed them in if they didn't get in the water straight away. Others recounted stories of school swimming carnivals at the baths and learning to dive off the old-fashioned timber diving tower.

The 1960s and early 70s, when my friends and I were learning to swim at Nedlands Baths, was the era before there were many chlorine pools in Perth – or anywhere in Western Australia. (We didn't get one in Bunbury until 1974, the same year we got Kentucky Fried Chicken, the town's first set of traffic lights, and Woolworths started selling Danish salami, which my father was very excited about.) So huge numbers of people in Perth learned to swim at Nedlands Baths and other timber baths on the Swan River.

We called our grandmother Bessa, the nickname my dad gave her instead of *bedstemor*, the Danish word for grandmother. My great-aunty's name was Gudren, but to us she was Aunty Las. The story behind how they came to Australia is an interesting one. The sisters were born in a small village in Denmark, Bessa in 1901 and Aunty Las in 1905. Both of them were keen to escape the confines of village life and in 1939 Aunty Las arrived in Perth. She'd left her husband in the village and come to Western Australia with another Danish man she had fallen in love with. In the early 1940s she had two children, Karen and Peter, and ended up marrying their father, Carl Pedersen.

My grandmother Edith left Denmark a number of years before Aunty Las to work as an au pair in France, where she met and married a Croatian man, Branko Vukelic and had my father, Paul. Branko was a journalist and in 1933 they moved to Japan where he worked for the French News Agency, Havas. It turned out he was also part of the most famous spy ring in Asia, run by Richard Sorge. Branko and my grandmother ended up breaking up, but when he got early warning that the Japanese were going to make a surprise attack on the US naval base at Pearl Harbour on 7 December 1941, he arranged for his former wife and son to get out of Japan. They couldn't go back to Denmark because it was occupied by the Nazis, so, with my great-aunty already in Perth, they got on a boat and arrived in Western Australia in October 1941.

In those early years in Perth, Aunty Las and Bessa taught dancing in winter and, from about 1943, taught swimming at the Claremont Baths, another timber enclosure on the Swan River. Their lessons included teaching the Holger Nielsen life-saving technique, a method of artificial respiration developed in Copenhagen by Holger Louis Nielsen, a physical fitness instructor in the Danish army. They also had a water ballet school inspired by the synchronised swimming style of Hollywood star Esther Williams.

When they took on the lease of the Nedlands Baths in 1953, Aunty Las and her husband and two children, and my grandmother, her new husband Chris Nielsen and my father, all moved into the accommodation at the baths. Carl and Chris weren't involved in the business of running the baths or the swimming school. Aunty Las and Bessa wanted to be independent and not rely on their husbands for financial security, so Bessa looked after the running of the baths while Aunty Las taught swimming and did the books.

The Nedlands Baths were quite a remarkable construction, made of jarrah timber, but by the mid to late 1960s, when I started going there, it was quite old and seemed to be under constant repair. Every season Bessa painted the whole of the baths. I remember watching in awe as this tanned, white-haired lady in very smart bathers climbed up a high ladder and did what seemed the equivalent of painting the Sydney Harbour Bridge!

To get to the baths you had to walk along the Nedlands jetty that stretched out into the Swan River. Before you reached the end where people were fishing, you'd turn right and continue along this narrow rickety timber pathway and after about 20 metres, the baths were on your left. On one corner of the façade was the famous red Coca-Cola sign, and further along the name NEDLANDS BATHS appeared in block letters along the top of the timber.

When we reached the entrance, we'd pay our five cents, go through the turnstiles and past the kiosk area where you could buy lollies from a big glass jar and Coke and Fanta in old-style bottles, which we were never allowed to have. Next to the entrance were the living quarters, and in front of us was this area of water surrounded by the timber enclosure. On one side of the deep end was an old-fashioned diving tower, and on the other side were small, very basic timber change cubicles.

There were gaps in between the planks on the rickety deck and aged six I was always worried I was going to fall through. Aunty Las's daughter-in-law Wendy told me that the constant movement of the timber with the weather meant the planks were always uneven. In winter they swelled with the damp and became a dark colour; in summer they shrank and became the bleached silver grey of weather-beaten jarrah. Wendy said children would lie on the warm dry timber and look down through the cracks and watch the parade of blowfish, crabs and stingrays in the water below.

I remember looking down through those gaps as I changed into my bathers in one of those small cubicles and seeing brown, mushroom-shaped jellyfish. We used to call them man-of-wars, but apparently they were brown jellyfish that increased in numbers when the river water was warmer in summer. There were masses of them and when you got in the water they would rub up against your arms, but fortunately they didn't seem to sting. If the tide was low there'd be this really strong smell of salty water, and because the Fremantle Doctor came in any time after lunch, that sea breeze would whisper through the cracks in the building and the gaps in the timber.

While Aunty Las was the main swimming teacher, on those weeks when my brother and sister and I were learning to swim, we would have private lessons with Bessa. The water always seemed quite cold and murky and full of those brown jellyfish and if it was low tide, we'd be three or four metres below the timber deck, which when I was little seemed a long way down. Apparently the water was murkier in winter when silt and heavy rain flowed down from the wine-growing areas up the river. By the end of summer, the tides from the Indian Ocean brought clearer, saltier water into the river as well as amazing fish, sometimes even chased by dolphins.

Bessa and Aunty Las had a very strict approach to teaching swimming. Bessa had this big bamboo stick and if you felt a bit tired and tried to hold on to the piers that were covered in barnacles, she'd hit your hand. Bessa and Aunty Las were different to other people's grandmothers and aunties. They were amazing women but they weren't soft. They gave us dark chocolate Toblerone as they thought milk chocolate was rubbish. It was a different era and both of them brought their background in calisthenics to the lessons. They'd done calisthenics as children in Denmark, and Bessa had taught it in Japan. They were stereotypically Danish in their straightforward approach, and had a strong ethos about being fit. They brought a philosophy of discipline and self-control to the Pedersen School of Swimming.

Our swimming lessons weren't really connected with having a good time, but afterwards we were allowed to choose some lollies from the big jar in the kiosk. Even though the baths always seemed to be in a state of disrepair and we rarely swam for fun, it still seemed an exotic place to me with these very European women living on the premises and running swimming, water ballet and diving schools. They both had strong accents and believed in ageing naturally, so they never dyed their hair. They rarely wore dresses but were stylish in their slacks suits with lots of silver jewellery, and they smoked, drank and put bets on at the TAB. The other thing that made it an exotic place to me as a little girl was that Aunty Las's daughter Karen was dating an Olympic swimmer who trained there.

My favourite thing about those baths was going there for family celebrations, which we did often – for birthdays, christenings and for Christmas. The living quarters reminded me of a big old timber boathouse. They were made of jarrah wood like the rest of the baths, and when you walked in there was one big room where they'd added a kitchen. At the other end were the bedrooms, which they'd created out of some of the original small change cubicles.

When the baths were closed to the public it was lovely having the place all to ourselves. They were actually quite a long way out on the river, and because there were all these playing fields near the foreshore, it was at least 400 metres to the closest building, so it seemed quite secluded. When I'd stay overnight, I'd lie there drifting off to sleep with the sounds of the water flowing underneath. It was beautiful. When it got dark, we'd walk out on those rickety timber planks and see the lights of the city reflected on the river and look across to Como, where my Aunty Las's son Peter used to row across to his high school. Later when my grandmother moved to a house down the road and Peter and his wife Wendy were living at the baths, their two little kids would ride their tricycles over the timber path, and I remember the sound of their Afghan dogs bounding over it, too.

We had all our big Danish Christmas celebrations there and everyone would be around the beautifully decorated tree on Christmas Eve. Instead of turkey we'd have pork, red cabbage and lots of potatoes, and rice pudding for dessert. We'd follow the Danish tradition of the youngest child giving out the first present. Everyone had to watch the unwrapping of each present and as we did, all the adults drank schnapps.

For thousands of Perth people, the Nedlands Baths was the place where they learned to swim, but for my family on the Danish side, it was our gathering place for all our important events. For my great-aunty and my grandmother, it offered a chance to make a new life in Australia. I don't think either of them would ever have imagined they would end up running a swimming school and living at a tidal baths on the Swan River. But they both revelled in making it a success. They enjoyed having control over it and the independence it gave them after their very restricted life in the little village in Denmark. Although they weren't sentimental women, they had a strong connection to the place and when they died in the 1980s we all knew where they'd want their ashes scattered – into the Swan River near those old timber baths, the place that had been their home and workplace for more than 20 years.

JO-ANNE LARTER

A water-lover in Launceston

Jo-Anne Larter spent her childhood in the 1960s and 70s in a part of Launceston not far from Cataract Gorge, a nature reserve by the South Esk River where a swimming pool had been built in 1937. Known as the First Basin Pool for its location beside the river basin, the pool was enlarged in 1950. In summer Jo-Anne went to the pool every afternoon after school with her mother and two sisters and later her younger brother.

O ur house in Frederick Street was just over the top of the hill from Cataract Gorge and our summer routine after school was to race home, get changed, and head over the hill to the gorge and the First Basin Pool. My dad worked long hours and interstate, so it was just Mum who took us there after school. At that stage she didn't drive, so we'd walk up the hill and through Arbour Park in our thongs with boards under our arms and into this beautiful bush setting at Cataract Gorge where there were wallabies, pademelons and all sorts of wildlife.

I still remember the excitement of reaching the top of the grassy slopes, where we could see the pool. Mum would be yelling, 'Don't run down the hill, don't run down the hill!' But we always did the mad dash to get to the pool. We'd swim and swim and then we'd sit on the concrete ledges around the pool and eat the tomato sandwiches Mum always made on fresh bread with salt and pepper and watch the sun going down over the hill. There'd be no music playing, no sounds, just the extraordinary quiet of that spectacularly beautiful place. Then Mum would drag us three girls back up over the hill and we'd all be complaining about the big trek. When we got home, we'd go straight to bed and the next afternoon after school we'd be back there again. It was just life as we knew it way back then. That was our summer routine from the time we were little tackers.

The pool was open from the first week of November through to Easter and it was always very cold in the water for the first swims of the season. We'd get in and jump out straight away and then get back in, even though we were freezing. On the walk home after those first couple of swims our teeth would be chattering, we'd have blue lips and our towels around our shoulders. But the next day, we'd be back. The pool was never heated but the beautiful thing was that being right down at the very bottom of the gorge, it didn't get a lot of wind, so during summer the pool could get quite warm, especially the shallow side.

The first pool that opened in 1937 was built to provide somewhere safe for children and inexperienced swimmers, as the First Basin was too deep for them. It proved very popular and in 1950 it was enlarged, and on the side closest to the basin a seven-lane, 55-yard pool was added. I've got the most beautiful photos of a horse and carriage taking the rocks out when the pool was initially being built, and one taken about 10 years later with all the girls standing around in their 1940s bathing suits. It was a fabulous pool because one side was deep for the big kids and the other side was shallow; a very narrow ledge about four inches wide separated the two. The shallow part was a semi-elliptical shape and the depth was only a couple of inches to about a foot, so it was a wonderful pool for little tackers. My sisters and I loved running through it and splashing each other.

When we were very little we were only allowed on the shallow side; the big excitement then was being allowed to run along the narrow ledge between the two pools. Then we were allowed to go in the shallow side of the deeper pool, where we'd play Marco Polo, and once we were able to swim we'd could go anywhere in that big kids' pool, even the deep end.

I loved being in the deep pool, but my favourite spot when I was a little kid was always on the left side of the shallow pool, where we could watch the big kids diving in. I would stand there in my favourite red and white polka-dot bikini with its frilly shorts and frilly straps, in awe of the big kids doing their big bombs and huge splashes. All the local kids came to the pool and we got to know everyone. They were our swimming buddies, our summer friends.

We didn't have any swimming lessons at the First Basin Pool but we were all water people in our family and we just seemed to pick it up, especially when Dad threw us in the deep end of Launceston's Windmill Hill Swimming Pool. We learned pretty fast after that, and with all the time we spent at the First Basin Pool we mastered floating and dog paddle and in the end we all became quite good swimmers. In our high school years, we did competitive swimming.

In our teenage years the big thing was graduating from the deep side of the pool and being able to swim in the basin – the natural waterhole in the South Esk River itself, where only the big kids went. Mum was always really thingy about it. The basin is quite deep and because we were all doing competitive swimming by that stage, she didn't want us being stupid and jumping off Hog's Bottom and hurting ourselves.

Hog's Bottom is quite a famous spot where there used to be a diving board, but because of safety issues it doesn't exist any more. It was just to the left of the pool, above a very deep part of the First Basin. A concrete area was built there, and on top of that was the diving board, and that's where everyone jumped into the basin. Even though Mum didn't want us to do it, of course I did, along with all my friends when I was about 14, leaping off Hog's Bottom and into the freezing, deep dark water of the basin. For the past nearly 70 years that progression from the shallow pool to the deep pool, then to the deep end and finally into the basin, has continued to be a rite of passage among the young in Launceston. It hasn't changed.

And every year the river would flood and flow into the pool and it would be completely underwater. We always came down to the gorge when it flooded, as the water would get wild and noisy and pour all over the pool and up over the grass we used to run down. Because my parents built and ran the chairlift at the gorge, we'd get to ride it back and forth from the south side to the north and get a wonderful view of the flood. I remember looking down and there was no blue pool. It had disappeared beneath the dark river water and branches, rocks and debris brought down with the flood.

Mostly the gorge flooded in winter, but I remember when I was about six, we had a summer flood. It was unusual for it to flood at that time of year and everyone in Launceston came to have a look. Nowadays the council empties the pool out and refills it quite quickly after a summer flood, but back then they didn't, so we couldn't swim there until the next year. I remember wanting to go there for a swim after school but we weren't allowed, so Mum had to find other activities for us as we were very active kids, and little terrors at times.

When I think back on those days at the First Basin Pool I get goosebumps and a warm and fuzzy feeling. At the pool we were allowed to run and play, fall over and hurt ourselves, get dunked by friends, throw things at each other and do water bombs. It was an idyllic way to grow up and we loved every bit of being there (except for the walk back up the hill) and we came back and did it all again the next day.

My love of water started at the First Basin Pool. I still remember the excitement I felt when we reached the gorge on those afternoons after school and looked down over this amazing landscape of bush and river that started forming millions of years ago, and the pool at the bottom of this large area of green grass and beautiful trees. There was something about the meeting of the green with the blue of the water in the pool, the river, the birds and the wildlife that I found peaceful as a kid. Whenever I returned there as an adult I always felt I'd come home.

DIANE FINGLETON

Escaping to the Spring Hill Baths

Diane Fingleton spent the first 13 years of her life in the late 1940s and 50s in the inner-city Brisbane suburb of Spring Hill. At that time, Spring Hill was considered a rough place full of brothels, SP bookies, gangsters and people struggling to pay their bills. But Diane and her four older brothers never felt scared. This was their community, made special by the close proximity of the Spring Hill Baths, Brisbane's first in-ground pool, built to replace floating river baths in 1886.

We didn't own our house at 490 Boundary Street but when I was little I thought we owned the Spring Hill Baths, as it was only a two-minute walk to get there down Boundary Street, past the International Hotel and into Torrington Street. We usually ran there because the ground was hot under our feet but later we had thongs before anyone else had them. Dad was a wharfie and I think he got them from a container he was unloading on the docks. They were a Japanese style and we were happy we had something before the other kids.

It cost sixpence to get into the pool and sometimes if the owner wasn't looking we got in for free. He never said anything or demanded we pay if he saw us in the pool. At the beginning of the season in September the water was like ice. Sometimes I got changed in the little timber sheds that surrounded the pool, but usually I'd run straight in and jump in the water. I had four older brothers, Harold, Tony, John and Ron and we were always racing to see who could be the first one to break the ice, then the first to the bottom and the first to swim to the end. I was the youngest and only girl and I'd be yelling, 'Oh I can't keep up,' or 'You're all bigger than me.' We were very compet-itive with each other but very close. Mum made us all incredibly close – us against the world.

Mum was very loving but Dad was a difficult man. He didn't drink for a long time and then he busted badly. When he'd been drinking and there was trouble at home, we'd escape to the pool. We'd be there morning, noon and night. I had a fantasy that Dad would get the lease one day and we'd live there. Mind you, the accompanying house was very tiny – tinier than our big old Queens-lander high up on stilts with verandahs at the front and back. But the pool house was two-storey and I thought that would be fun. Dad did think about it at one stage but he said he'd never get it because he had a criminal history. I'm not sure if he was rejected but the man who got it was Eric Potter, whose daughters swam with us. He was a very cranky man. You'd walk in and say, 'Good morning Mr Potter. Mr Potter?' and you'd get nothing in return. There were terrible stories of him teaching children to swim and keeping them in the water with a broom handle and not letting them out till the parents came to see it. But Dad probably wouldn't have had the patience for it. And what if he'd started drinking? The pub was just across the road, so it was a risk and Mum probably knew it.

We had no concept that the pool was historic. To us, it was our haven, our playground where we had fun but also where we developed our swimming abilities. The baths were hidden behind a two-storey painted brick building, and from the street you might not have known there was a pool inside except that across the triangular pediment at the top were the words: '1886, Municipal Public Baths, James Hipwood Mayor'. Mayor Hipwood opened the baths and apparently after his official duties were over, he was the first one to dive in.

The pool was just over 25 yards in length and around the edge were timber change cubicles, which in my day were a cream colour, not multi-coloured like today. There were quirky signs like, 'Men must not loiter at this end of the pool' and 'Ladies only this side', and something about 'spitting and smoking' being 'strictly prohibited'. In one corner was the original foundation stone from 1886. It never occurred to us how old it was, but we knew it was special.

There was no grassed area to sunbake in, but we loved the open roof and if it rained we swam in the rain and we liked that. Upstairs was a gallery area for spectators, but years before they'd moved the swimming carnivals to the Valley pool, so there was never anyone up there. But we raced around there and my brothers used to swing along the pipes across the top where the stands are and drop down into the pool when the bloke who had the lease wasn't looking. You didn't dive from there because it was too shallow.

We made a game out of anything. We'd dive off the diving board and catch a ball, dive for a penny and see who was the first to get it, race from one end to the other and see how long we could stay under water. We'd swim between each other's legs and, after seeing Esther Williams' movies with her spectacular synchronised swimming, we'd all try and recreate her moves in the water. The pool was our natural environment and my hair was always wet. I had long hair and there was no conditioner then but Mum would comb it and I would go off with beautiful plaits.

I don't remember learning to swim, though at one stage we had lessons at Bill Fleming's, but our swimming just seemed to improve naturally because we were always at the pool. We were a very sporty, athletic family. My brothers would con me into playing cricket and touch football with them. If we'd picked up tennis racquets we might have gone down that track instead of swimming.

Mum never came to the pool and we rarely saw her in a pair of togs. She knew we were all good swimmers so she never worried about us and she got to have a break from us. Dad never came either, until one day one of the boys convinced him to come. He didn't get in the water. He just stood on the side and watched. Tony and John had a race and afterwards Dad said to them, 'Can you always swim like that?' And they said, 'Sure.' After that he threw himself into training us – the boys more than me. He went a bit softer on me. If I said I was tired and I didn't want to do any more laps, he'd say he'd give me sixpence if I did four more laps. So I did and usually I bought some lollies with the sixpence. My brothers used to go straight into the fish and chip shop next door to our house and get sixpence worth of chips and a Pepsi.

Dad took training us very seriously, even though he didn't know anything about swimming. He wasn't able to show us how to improve our strokes but he would be banging on our bedroom doors at six o'clock in the morning to get us down to the pool. He'd have us tapering down and taking vitamins and for some reason we'd eat baked beans at four o'clock before a race. The downside was if you didn't win he wouldn't talk to you.

We were members of the Valley Club at the pool down the road in Fortitude Valley and Mum and Dad came to the Wednesday night carnivals. If you won Dad would yell out, 'You little beauty!' somewhere up in the stands. But he wasn't exuberant after that and he never said, 'You did well tonight,' or 'I'm really proud of you.' I used to think that only happened in the movies. There was none of that and if he was drunk he might say something else and one time he fell into the pool. The next morning he'd have us up at six and back training at Spring Hill Baths.

Dad lived through us and our swimming. We won a lot, especially John and Tony. Tony won a silver medal in the 220 yards backstroke at the 1962 Empire Games in Perth, and our house was overflowing with trophies. Even though we had issues at home and we didn't have much money, I grew up with the idea that we were a special family because of our swimming success.

When I was about 13 we got notice that we had to leave our house at 490 Boundary Street because it was being sold. Mum said she walked Queen Street to try and get a mortgage but they wouldn't give her one because they said Dad's job as a wharfie made him a seasonal worker. When we ended up in Holland Park in a Housing Commission house, we thought our throats had been cut. We were city kids and in Holland Park we had long walks to the buses. We missed the Spring Hill community, the access to the city, our friends and, of course, the pool. The Spring Hill Baths were a joyous, fun, safe place where my brothers and I were each other's friends, where we could have absolute freedom, where there was always someone to play with, and where we were known at the Flying Fingletons!

Champions
of the pool

PRIYA COOPER

From Kalamunda to the Paralympics

Priya Cooper spent a lot of time in the water when she was growing up in the hills above Perth from the mid 1970s to the early 1990s. In pools she did therapy for her cerebral palsy, had fun with her brother and cousins, and expertly executed a handstand – something it was not possible for her to do on dry land. She also trained and competed in indoor and outdoor pools, big and small, on her journey to becoming a gold medal winning Paralympian. But her favourite pools were close to home: in her family's backyard, and at the Kalamunda Aquatic Centre in the suburb next door to her Lesmurdie home.

The first pool I swam in as a little kid was my family's backyard pool. It was an above-ground pool with that blue liner and a ladder that came all the way down the outside and into the pool. My brother and I spent a lot of time in that pool, and all day when our cousins came to visit. We were very close to my mother's side of the family and pretty much every weekend we'd have cousins at our house. When we'd have a big rellie bash everyone – parents and kids – would get in that pool. Sometimes when the adults got in we'd get out because they'd ruin our fun. Other times we'd swim in our cousins' pools because four out of five of Mum's brothers and sisters had backyard pools. Being outdoors and in the water was a big part of my childhood.

The Kalamunda Pool came into my life when I was about five or six, as that's where all the swimming lessons – vacation and school programs and Learn to Swim – were held in the area where I lived. It was a big outdoor aquatic centre with a 50-metre pool, two shallow children's pools, grassed areas, a canteen and two huge water slides. Those slides were really popular, but not for me. I climbed up there once, which was a huge effort, and afterwards I knew I didn't want to do that again. It was always stinking hot on the days I went to swimming lessons and we'd have to line up in a row and sit on the hot concrete that would burn your bum. Then we'd be allocated a teacher from a group of ladies wearing vests with numbers on their chests and we'd go off for our lesson in the cold water. I started out in one of the kids' pools, where the water would have been up to my parents' knees, and I always remember the smell of the hot chips as we did our lessons.

After a few rounds of those lessons, I moved on to the shallow end of the 50-metre pool and then the deep end, where I did my junior certificate. I had been scared of the deep water because it was pretty challenging for me as my legs didn't work very well. They just dangled and I couldn't kick, so I had to use my arms and upper body to tread water and keep afloat. To pass the junior certificate I had to go into the deep end and swim through a hoop. I remember how excited I was when I swam under the water and through the hoop. Once I'd achieved that junior certificate it was like *wow*! I loved swimming from the beginning but the deep end had been a bit scary, so it was great to conquer that fear.

Swimming was part of the therapy I did for my cerebral palsy but I quite enjoyed it because water gave me more freedom than I had on land. I had a very positive mother who always encouraged me to do all sorts of things, like play netball and do ballet, which was great. For a while I was goal keeper in the netball team and I'd try and defend a bit, but as we got older you needed to do more than just stand there, so they made me captain and I encouraged the team from the sidelines. I did whatever I could to be involved. Swimming was an activity I could do and was more of a level playing field for me. Doing handstands was something all the girls did when I was a kid, which I could never really do. In the pool, my friends would say, 'Let's have a handstand competition,' and in the water I could join in and be part of the group. I quite enjoyed that, and we'd do somersaults too.

In Lesmurdie we were 30 minutes' drive away from any major shops or services, so unless you got your parents to drive you, which didn't happen very often, most of our recreation was done locally. Kalamunda had the only two local places to go to – the pool or the roller skating rink, which was next door. The Kalamunda Pool was the meeting place where we'd hang out with our friends. Our parents would drop us there at 9 a.m. with $10 or $15 and you'd stay there till 5 p.m. Later we all rode our bikes down there.

There was a big grassed hill off to the side at the pool and we all used to congregate there and people would put coconut oil on themselves and there'd be that mixture of coconut oil, hot chips and the smell of the pool. I don't think we had any shade and we used to stay there all day – sitting and talking and eating junk. I got some backlash through the years and a bit of bullying, but I always had a core group of friends who I still have. We were never in the popular group but that didn't worry us – we did our own thing and enjoyed ourselves at the pool.

The Kalamunda Pool was where we'd have our school swimming carnivals, which I was always involved in. I was quite a good swimmer but I was never good enough because I was competing against able-bodied swimmers. My school, which was both a primary and high school, had a pool and in the lead-up to the carnival anyone who wanted to was invited to train there in the mornings. It was just this little 25-metre pool that had algae in it and was only six lanes. It was down near the oval on the primary side of the school. I decided it was something I could be involved in.

So, I went there and trained and they ended up giving me my own lane, which was quite nice. I was part of the swim team in that way and I would train with them. When it came to the carnival I would be in Division F but that didn't bother me. When it came to competitions I would never make the inter-school or anything like that, until one year towards the end of high school they put me in a relay, so that was really good. It was probably tokenistic but I didn't care as it gave me a chance to be part of it.

I swam and swam and swam in those late primary school years and into high school – at home, at the Kalamunda Pool, and at the school pool – but with no real direction. And then I started training at the Maida Vale Pool down the hill, which was an indoor 25-metre pool with not a lot of room on either side of the pool. The air was so thick because it was such a small place. It was heated and had a very strong smell of chlorine. As soon as you opened the door you were sweating because it was very warm in there. It was so shallow at one end that your fingers would touch the bottom when you were doing freestyle, and you had to be really careful when you tumble-turned.

When I was training at Maida Vale a sports teacher at my school suggested I try out for people with disabilities sport. At that stage it wasn't part of my world because I didn't know it existed. But that teacher put me in touch with the right people and that was the start of my progression to becoming a Paralympian and going to the 1992

Barcelona Games and then Atlanta and finally Sydney in 2000. After the 1992 Paralympics I moved from the little Maida Vale Pool to become part of the squad at the Swan Park Leisure Centre at Midvale, my training base for the next five or so years.

When I started competing at the international level I swam in some amazing pools – the awesome pool at the Atlanta Paralympics, the one at the Barcelona Paralympics with the spectacular view over the city, and a fantastic outdoor pool in Malta where the world championships were held – when a massive storm came through they locked us all inside and bought us pizza.

They were spectacular competition pools, but my favourite ones will always be our above-ground backyard pool, where I spent so much time with my extended family as a child, and the Kalamunda Pool because it was part of my social upbringing. I did swimming carnivals there and had fun with my friends before I ever knew that pools would be such a big part of my life.

From a young age I always wanted to achieve something. I just didn't know what it was going to be. It worked out to be swimming. When I was in the middle of Paralympic swimming I didn't think about how it was going to end and how it would shape my career and my whole life. I just loved the training, challenging myself and the actual physical side, and competing in all those pools in Australia and around the world, from Perth's Superdrome to the ones at Hornsby and Manly in Sydney where I lived and trained before the 2000 Olympics. But my fondest memories are those childhood days up on the grassy hill at the Kalamunda Pool enjoying a bucket of hot chips with my friends.

SHANE GOULD

Learning about life at Pymble

During her competitive swimming career Shane Gould swam in many beautiful pools, including the iconic North Sydney Pool and Munich's Olympia-Schwimmhalle, where as a 15-year-old she won three gold medals, a silver and a bronze at the 1972 Olympic Games. But the pool she formed the strongest connection with was an ugly duckling indoor pool set among small office blocks in Pymble on Sydney's upper north shore. For seven months of the year, from 1970 to 1973, she trained in the busy lanes of the 25-metre pool run by her coach Forbes Carlile and his wife Ursula.

In 1970 we moved back to Sydney after living in Fiji and Brisbane, where my father worked for airline companies. My parents decided to settle in West Pymble because it was between Ryde pool and the Carlile Swimming Centre at Pymble, the two pools where my coach

Forbes Carlile was based. In the warmer months I trained at Ryde, and at Pymble from about April to October. I trained in the T-shaped 50-metre pool at the Ryde Swimming Centre, which was very cold at the beginning and end of the season, but it was nice to be outdoors and get a suntan and breathe fresh air. My Ryde pool memories are also associated with the Saturday club races that my sisters and I did, but I preferred the connection with the squad at Pymble and the intensity of the training in the enclosed space.

It wasn't necessarily that I liked the pool, as it was very utilitarian and had very little aesthetics to it. Frank O'Neill had established it as a learn-to-swim centre in the late 1950s and Forbes and Ursula leased it from him in 1966 till it was closed down in 1983 and redeveloped into offices. It was the only indoor pool in the area for all that time and thousands of local children learned to swim there and more serious swimmers like me did squad. It was basically an industrial shed but I had a relationship with it because it was where I went to train, before school and back again in the afternoons, five days a week.

I loved training. I especially liked the early mornings; the whole ritual of waking up and going outside, the glow of the sunrise on the horizon and the fresh, cool air and getting picked up or Mum or Dad driving me to the pool. When we arrived, I'd tumble out of the car and hurry through the two sets of glass doors, lugging my bag and my school uniform on a coathanger. I'd pass the little kiosk where we bought lollies, leave my stuff in the change rooms and walk to the end where the coaches wrote the training programs on a blackboard. We started training at a quarter to five in the mornings and often there was steam rising off the water. Condensation would drip down from the roof and off the girders and the glass windows would fog up. It was very atmospheric.

The pool was very crowded and the water could get pretty turbulent. There'd be eight, 10, sometimes 12 people in a lane in a 25-metre pool, so you had to be really careful when you were passing each other, be really aware of space and tuck your arm in so it didn't get whacked by a big strong guy. The lane ropes were just corks on a rope and sometimes the water was horribly smelly when they didn't get the chemical balance right and the chlorine stung your eyes. It was before we wore goggles all the time so we were always using Murine and our skin got really dry, especially scaly calves, so we always had a kit of baby oil.

In the mornings Forbes was usually in the office and his assistant coach Tom Green ran the squad. In the afternoons, Forbes would be standing by the blackboard running the show, chalk in one hand and his stopwatch in the other. He was never really a people person; he was more of a scientist and I think that's probably why we got on. I had really professional relationships with Forbes and Tom Green because we were all in the business of swimming fast. I used to plan year to year with my swimming. Some of that was my parents' strategising, as they were pretty rational people, but when I started breaking

Australian records when I was 13 and a half, I knew I was good. The next big thing, two years later, was the Munich Olympics, so I was working towards that.

I was really in my body when I was training. I was very physically aware of my structures, my capacities and the pleasure I could get from my body moving and exerting itself. I loved the deep breathing and those really strong exhales – my lungs expanding to their capacity and the strains of my muscles, and then getting to the end and stopping to rest and recover within 20, 30, 40 seconds and be back to normal breathing again. I loved pushing myself as hard as I could till I was gasping for air and feeling the strain on my muscles, especially my shoulders. At the time we had nylon suits because lycra wasn't invented till 1973. I remember putting my hands on my waist and feeling my hip bones and the flatness of my stomach but also the curve of my waist, like an awakening to my femaleness.

In between sets we'd have breaks and we'd talk and tell jokes and play all those games teenagers play with each other – stirring and teasing. There were a couple of girls my age in the lane but mostly older guys who were 17, 18, 19, 20 and one of them was my boyfriend. We were quite bunched up together in the lane so you could brush skin and touch and there was the spark of sexual attraction. It was a social education being with people of different ages, particularly listening to the guys' conversations about what they got up to on the weekend, which was totally foreign to me. I learned a lot about older people's lifestyles and about things that can get you into trouble, like drinking or driving someone else's car when you shouldn't have, or staying out later than you should have and having to lie to cover certain behaviour.

If we were doing longer distances, usually I would lead the lane. I'd make the guys work hard and they hated me for it. I was very competitive and a lot of them would say, 'Oh, you're going too fast, Shane – we can't keep up,' and I'd think, *Yes*. I knew I was learning a life lesson about people, about how to be competitive and how you can psyche someone out and put them off their game.

Quite often the guys weren't as serious as I was with the training and they didn't put in the effort. Or they'd go off at the wrong time and cause traffic jams and Forbes would get frustrated. Sometimes I'd do something deliberately naughty to keep in with them and Forbes would growl at me and say, 'Get out.' You had to stay out for 10 minutes and then you could come back in again. But being naughty didn't come naturally to me and I didn't like doing it. I was a good girl and I wanted to be a good swimmer and I was prepared to train hard to get there. It was more important to me to get the training miles in than to be socially accepted. It isolated me a bit but I was prepared to do that to achieve what I wanted in swimming.

I spent a lot of time in that pool – probably more than 25 hours a week – swimming four miles in the morning and about three in the afternoon. I had a relationship with the building, the water, the steam and the fog and the different dynamics according to who was there and what was going on. I had a sense of place there and I felt comfortable, at home, safe and relaxed. But the pool didn't shape my success. It was what I did in that space – the hard work – that led to me being the only person, male or female, to hold every world freestyle record from 100 metres to 1500 metres and the 200-metres individual medley simultaneously, in 1971 and 1972.

DANIEL KOWALSKI

From little pools big champions grow

During his competitive swimming career, Daniel Kowalski swam in many grand aquatic centres, but it was a tiny pool in the suburbs of Adelaide where the foundations of his achievements were laid. In 1981, a year after he'd moved to Australia from Singapore, the six-year-old started training at the Seaton Swim Centre, not far from his family's Henley Beach home. In the stuffy confines of that five-lane pool, his coach identified the 1500-metres freestyle as Daniel's perfect race.

My sister and I didn't have proper swimming lessons when we were living in South-East Asia, but Mum and Dad taught us at various country club pools where all the expats hung out. When we arrived in Australia in 1981, we could both hold our own in the water and our parents were comfortable we were safe. My sister is two and a half years older than me and after she'd swum in a school carnival at the Henley and Grange saltwater pool, a local coach asked if she wanted to do squad at the Seaton Swim Centre. I tagged along with her and it went from there.

The outside of the Seaton Swim Centre was this plain, flat-roofed, painted concrete building in the middle of a suburban street. Inside was a tiny 25-metre indoor pool that had four lanes, but they squeezed five lanes out of it. I started doing squad there when I was about six. My sister did it for a couple of years but then it was just me. It was a very dark and dingy pool and the lanes were very, very narrow so you would continually hit people's hands in your lane and in the next lane. You never wanted to get into lane one because that was the fifth lane they'd jammed in and it was very narrow. You could never dive properly because the edge of the pool wasn't flat. It was lipped so you were always having to lean backwards, grip your toes onto that raised edge and hope you didn't slip. In winter when they opened the back door, the fog within the pool would be so thick that some of the naughty kids would hide in a corner and the coach wouldn't see them and they'd miss their laps. That always used to make me angry.

When I was quite young I was doing six or seven sessions a week, mornings and afternoons, and as I got older we'd do anywhere between three kilometres and five kilometres. I loved training. I loved the discipline of it and the challenge and I was forever recreating races in my head that I'd seen on TV. At that stage I was still doing all the strokes and we'd do a lot of medley training, so I mainly re-enacted Jon Sieben swimming the 200-metres butterfly and Rob Woodhouse in the 400-metres medley.

From a very young age I was acutely aware of the history and tradition of swimming in Australia, and being new to the country – very much being an immigrant – I wanted to fit in, so that drove me in many ways. I also loved swimming. I loved how I could be lost in my own thoughts, but at other times I'd use the time in the pool to study in my head and go through my homework. Multitasking in the pool. When we stopped at the end of the pool after a set, my friends would be there and I always enjoyed it when we'd talk – maybe about a surf carnival coming up on the weekend or a movie we were all going to see. The other kids I swam with were my closest friends. We all did surf lifesaving at the same club and some of us went to the same school. It was all intertwined.

On the way out after squad we'd always get a couple of red frogs from the kiosk, which at the time seemed very big but was probably tiny. When we walked into the car park after it had been raining, all the parents would be waiting in their cars to take us home, and I remember it would be really muddy on the ground. The first job I ever had was at the Seaton Swim Centre and on Sundays I'd clean the pool with scrubbing brushes. Sometimes I also cleaned the toilets, but not very often. I'd be there for two hours and I was paid $20.

I got moved up to the big squad pretty quickly when I was quite young, so I was in lanes with guys who were five, sometimes 10, years older than me. In the early days I was scared of some of those big guys because they would threaten to flush my head down the toilet and things like that. I never wanted to go to the toilet because of that. They were intimidating but eventually they backed off when I started beating them.

My father did Masters Swimming in the same pool on a Monday and Wednesday night and as I got out of the pool he'd get in. Mum would be waiting to pick me up in the car park. When I look back, the commitment of my parents was amazing, getting me to morning and afternoon training and taking me to all the events. Once a month on a Friday night we'd have club races and afterwards all the families would gather for a barbeque on the concrete and grass area out the back. We'd do the races and then we'd eat and then all the kids would play in the pool while the parents had quite a lot to drink.

The next morning we'd see each other at training and then we'd all be doing nippers at Grange Beach together. We were quite a close group that included Sarah Ryan and Ryan Mitchell, and the three of us all qualified for the Atlanta Olympic Games in 1996. Our coach at the Seaton Swim Centre in the early days was David James, and the program he ran in that tiny pool laid the foundations for Sarah, Ryan and me to win Olympic medals at either Atlanta, Sydney or Athens.

At one stage our coach bought a Tarago so he could drive us to the main swimming centre in North Adelaide on the other side of the city, so we could train in a

50-metre pool. We had to be in the water at 5 a.m., so we'd have to be at Seaton at 4.30 to be picked up. It was tough going getting up at a quarter past four when you were doing high school. That pool in North Adelaide was a complete contrast to the Seaton pool. When we got there we were all like, 'Wow, look at us.' It was an indoor pool but it was so big and bright. A massive complex with a 50-metre pool, a diving pool, various kids' pools – when I was young the place seemed huge.

Every major squad in Adelaide had two lanes at that pool, which highlights how small Adelaide was, especially in the late 1980s and early 90s. We were a small squad from a tiny pool, but at State meets we'd perform above our weight. When we were all 13, we went to age nationals and we won both club relays, and two of my training partners won individual races – Karl Phillips won the 100-metres freestyle and Kriston Chrisakis won the 100 breaststroke. There was one year, 1992, when I was 16, nearly 17, our club got in the top 10 in the point-score.

The Seaton pool is where I got my work ethic, and one of the things that David James did very well was to get me to realise that physically I was never going to be an imposing figure in the pool. He stressed that I needed to learn how to be technically the best I could possibly be, as that would be the way I could become a great swimmer. He really impressed on me the importance of technique, and so I built from that. He also realised that the 1500 freestyle was probably my only 'go-to' event if I was going to have any hope of achieving my dream of one day representing Australia. I wasn't good enough at sprinting. I couldn't do breaststroke and my shoulders didn't like butterfly, so the 1500 was my only hope. In 1990, within six months of my decision to concentrate on it, Glen Housman unofficially broke the world record and Kieren Perkins came on the scene.

I was very aware of all the long-distance swimmers who had come before, as I did all my school projects on the Olympics. So I knew about Stephen Holland and all the way back to Boy Charlton. Once I started focusing on the 1500 metres, my coach put me in one of the end lanes by myself at Seaton pool, and I did a fair bit of work on my own, swimming up and down doing the sets he wanted me to do. Earlier on, the fast lane in the middle of the pool had been my favourite spot, but later it became those end lanes which I had all to myself.

I kept training at that little pool in Seaton until 1992 when I turned 17 and my family moved to the Gold Coast for my swimming. I trained at the Miami Swim Club, which was so different to the Seaton pool in many ways. Miami was an eight-lane 50-metre pool, outdoors, and the weather was perfect. I had hundreds of training partners, as opposed to the small number at the Seaton Swim Centre, and there was a whole different level of intensity to the training. It was chalk and cheese.

From 1994 I spent a couple of years training with Bill Nelson at the old State Swimming Centre on Batman Avenue in Melbourne, and then at the new Melbourne Sports and Aquatic Centre at Albert Park. In that period I won three medals at the Atlanta Olympic Games, including silver in the 1500-metres freestyle. After the games, when my coach ended up quitting, I moved to the pool at the Australian Institute of Sport in Canberra, which I hated. It was too much like being in training camp mode 24/7. I was also dealing with a lot of personal stuff and just being in Canberra on my own wasn't healthy for me, so I went back to the Gold Coast where my parents were. I continued training until the Sydney Olympics in 2000 and was part of the 4 × 200-metre freestyle relay that won gold.

I owe a lot of what I achieved to the Seaton Swim Centre and I will always have fond memories of that place. I'm proud of the fact that there were three of us – Sarah, Ryan and me – who came from that tiny, tiny pool to all become Olympic medallists. As Paul Kelly, another South Australian, sang, 'From little things big things grow.'

LAURIE LAWRENCE

Smashing records in Townsville

If Laurie Lawrence hadn't suffered from a bronchial condition as a child and had part of one lung removed when he was 10, he might never have ended up living at Townsville's Tobruk Memorial Baths. But following his operation he was advised that he should swim to improve his remaining lung function. This led to his father becoming manager of the circa-1950 art deco baths, named in memory of members of the Australian forces who died at the siege of Tobruk in North Africa in World War II.

D ad wasn't the biggest man, and when he was playing football in Winton in central-west Queensland, the team called him Stumpy. He'd worked as a shearer's cook, a publican, a taxi driver, and at one stage he was a chook farmer. He'd had a colourful career, but after my operation he looked around for jobs that might help my breathing. Anyway, he got the job managing the

Tobruk Memorial Baths, and in 1952, when I was 11, we moved in.

The baths were right on The Strand, on the foreshore in Townsville, and out the front were four big palm trees that kids used to carve their initials in – *Jack loves Jill* or *Bill loves Bonnie*. Just beyond the palm trees was the entrance to the baths, quite a striking blue and white two-storey pavilion with three etched glass panels with fish and sea motifs above the doors. Once you went through the entrance and into the foyer, there was a little door on the right-hand side that took you upstairs to our accommodation. As you walked in, there was a kitchenette and just off that was a bathroom. There were a further two rooms – one of which my mother and father used and then the middle bedroom my two sisters and I shared. There was a balcony outside, where there was a toilet. It was pretty cramped accommodation but that didn't matter to me as a young kid. It was fantastic living at that pool.

It was just sunny days. I'd walk up the hill to school at the Christian Brothers, then afternoons I was down at the pool playing games. Old George Marshall who worked on the wharves used to come down and teach swimming. He helped teach me to swim and then I got into the squad and I started swimming up and down. I loved getting in the water and playing piggie, swimming across the pool, diving down to the bottom, and with all my mates we'd go off the diving boards. There were two diving boards at the deep end – a small one and a high one, and I'd relish the time I spent bomb diving off that big board.

Just beyond the Tobruk Baths was an ocean pool. It had been created by hitting rails from old railway lines into the mud all the way around to make an enclosure. The rails were held together with pieces of timber on the top. They were pretty narrow, so it was a bit like walking a tightrope, but I enjoyed walking around the top of that swimming enclosure and lowering my crab pots into the water. I caught many feeder crabs off those old rails at that ocean pool. Occasionally I'd swim in there, but I preferred the water in the Tobruk Baths.

I was a bit of a cricket fanatic and I'd bowl a cricket ball on the concrete area on the side of the pool near the women's dressing sheds. You couldn't use a bat, but I'd get a cricket ball and put a tin can down the other end and bowl and try and hit the tin. It was all fun stuff and I'd do it over and over again to improve my bowling.

In 1956, the Australian Olympic team decided to do their winter training at our pool in the warmer Townsville climate. All the town was asked if they could board one of these Olympic swimmers. Dad said we would and we were given Jon Henricks.

Then it was even more crowded in our two-bedroom place, but Jon Henricks didn't mind. He was a fine young man who finished up an Olympic champion. I clearly remember his short cropped blond hair, his enormous appetite, and having to make room so he could squeeze into our little unit. I think we probably ended up putting a bed out on the balcony for him, which wasn't a big balcony, but it overlooked the children's pool and the

55-yard pool. Every single year afterwards, Jon Henricks sent a Christmas card to my father, and when Dad passed away, he sent the Christmas card to me. He married an American and was very successful not only in the swimming pool but as a businessman. And he was a wonderful, wonderful fella.

A couple of my best-ever memories are from when Jon Henricks was staying with us and the trial swimming events were being held at Tobruk Baths before the Melbourne Olympic Games. For a number of weeks, all the great swimmers were training at our pool – Jon Henricks, Dawn Fraser, John Devitt, Lorraine Crapp, Murray Rose, David Theile and more. I loved watching them go through their paces and collecting their autographs.

The afternoon before the trials, two huge cranes lifted two small grandstands onto the grass on one side of the pool to cater for the numbers that were going to come and watch. The pool became like a colosseum with seats all around, down the far end and up in the permanent grandstand. That night while the racing was on I had my own private balcony up the top. I looked over and watched world record after world record broken. I don't think I've ever had a better view at any swimming pool ever in my life.

I witnessed numerous Australian and world records set and watched Dawn Fraser and Lorraine Crapp break five minutes for the 400 freestyle. The atmosphere was unbelievable. The stands were packed on both sides and the pool was bathed in light. The crowd reacted to every world record and sometimes there were two world records within the one race.

In the middle of the races there was a break and a couple of divers who used to come up to Tobruk Baths to train put on clown costumes and did a comedy routine off the high diving board. They did all sorts of backflips and somersaults and ran out and pretended to jump off the end but missed the board and flopped in to the water. Dad had a race too. He'd told everyone he could beat one of the sprinters over 55 yards so he invited one of them – it may have been Jon Henricks – to race. Dad finished up getting one of those lifesaver reels they use in the ocean to rescue people. He put it around his belly and on the word '*Go!*' a group of his mates down the other end started winding him in. He took in so much water he nearly drowned himself, but it was fun times.

It was a fantastic night and that team of Australian swimmers turned out to be our most successful in history. Just over a month after that night of records, I listened to those Australian swimmers win eight out of 13 gold medals at the Melbourne Olympic Games. I heard it all on my crackly radio sitting in the foyer as I sold entries to the pool.

My sisters Kay and Denise were good swimmers like me and they enjoyed the pool too. After hours we had it all to ourselves and it was great cooling off on those hot and humid North Queensland nights. When we were the only ones there, we were the kings and queens of the pool where all those Olympians had trained and competed. I loved being around that water, playing piggy, jumping on and off those diving boards and being in the kiosk where I could eat all the chips and sip on the drinks.

Unfortunately, when I was 15 my mother and father parted ways and I went with my mother down to Brisbane and finished my schooling there. But every holiday I'd go north. The pool would draw me back and I'd stay with my father. After I finished school I went to teachers' college and did my teaching diploma and physical education diploma. I played rugby union for the Wallabies on a tour to New Zealand in 1964. When I came back I was transferred to Toowoomba, but I got very sick there with my lung complaint, so I resigned from the Queensland Education Department.

I had no job so I went back to Townsville and Dad, and started teaching kids to swim for a living. I learned how to teach swimming when I did my teaching diploma and physical education diploma. I'd stand in the Tobruk pool with a big straw hat and a long-sleeved shirt to protect myself from the sun and I'd take class after class of kids. The Education Department used to send in 30 kids every half hour. They'd come in for 10 lessons in a row every day and it was amazing what you could teach those kids in consecutive lessons. I also coached kids at that pool and we produced a few state champions.

I stayed with Dad at the Tobruk pool, teaching and coaching, until the late 1960s. He continued managing the baths into his seventies until eventually he retired and went to live on Magnetic Island across the ocean from the pool. In the early 1970s when my coaching career took off, I moved to Sydney and later to Brisbane and trained world record holders and Olympic champions like Stephen Holland, Tracey Wickham, Jon Sieben and Duncan Armstrong. Over the past more than 50 years, I've worked at many different pools, but the Tobruk Baths will always hold special memories for me – as a teenager living there, as a young man teaching and coaching, and as the place where my passion for swimming began.

Country
pools

LEAH PURCELL

Dancing in the water at Murgon

When Leah Purcell was growing up in Murgon in
south-west Queensland in the 1970s and 80s, she
often joined her mob at Ficks Crossing, a section of
the Barambah Creek that ran through the district.
She dipped her toes in the water and waded into
the shallows in her sandshoes, but she rarely swam
for fear the Mundagutta (the rainbow serpent in her
grandmother's Gunggari language) would get her.
Instead she cooled off in the chlorine water at the
Murgon Jubilee Pool, named to honour the town's
sixtieth jubilee in 1964.

We thought we were pretty spesh in Murgon because
we had the big meatworks, the best flavoured milk,
and a 50-metre pool with a really deep, deep end. All the
other towns nearby, like Wondai and Goomeri, only had
25-metre pools, but ours was Olympic length – and we
had a grandstand, a huge grassed area, shade and trees,

a table tennis table and, in the 1980s, a slippery slide. We also had a diving board, and my brother would dive off it and carry on and perform. It's gone now because of public liability. Near the pump room there was a concrete area that was textured, so it was lovely to scratch your back on, and when our towels were so wet from being in and out of the water all day, we'd lie down on it and warm up. When they opened up a canteen we got very excited because we could get hot chips – chlorine and hot chips! We had surfies, too – the flavoured ice you could buy for 15 cents.

Back in the day it cost 20 cents to get into the pool, so to earn the money I mowed Mum's lawn. We had an old Queenslander house on a double block – a massive block, which we rented from the Aboriginal Housing. With the big, heavy Victa mower I'd make patterns in the grass and pretend they were highways, roads and houses, listening to the 1980s 'Top 40 Countdown' on my transistor strapped to my back. But on this one day, everyone was meeting at the pool, so I wanted to get the mowing done quickly. I said to Mum, 'Can I do up to the clothesline?' and she said, 'Do to the back laundry.' I ran to get it done and then Mum gave me the 20 cents in copper coins, but when I got to the pool I counted only 19 cents. I said to the manager, 'Mate, I just mowed the lawn to get here – can I pay that one cent later?' and he said, 'Oh, go in.'

The pool was the big meeting ground, the safe place in Murgon where all the white kids, us kids from the five blackfella families in town, and the kids from

Cherbourg – which used to be the Barambah Aboriginal Mission – all congregated. The Cherbourg kids had a different energy and some of the white kids were scared of them. They were a lot louder and prouder and had the attitude, 'If I want to dive off that diving board I won't go to the back of the line.'

There was racism in Murgon but I never saw any Aboriginal kids being turned away from the pool. I remember a few glances from some of the white mothers thinking, *We're in the same water as them*, but looking back, the pool was the only place in town that it seemed okay for everyone to be just doing their stuff. There were a lot of white girls hooking up with black boys and the pool became lover's lane. On really hot days you could barely swim a metre for running into people because everyone was at the pool.

I loved the water and even though it was chlorine, it felt velvety running through my hands. I'd play little games like making a bubbling noise across the top of the water with my mouth, pretending I was a speed boat rescuing people. It sounded so cool and I thought I was so clever. Sometimes I'd be alone after my friends had gone home and I'd dive under and get lost in the depths. Then I'd scare myself and think they'd let the shark from *Jaws* out in the pool and then I'd think, *No, no, no, not that game – that's the Mundagutta. That's in the creek, not in the pool.*

In swimming lessons in Grade 1, we had to float over the top of the star on the bottom of the little pool, the toddlers' pool, and see how long we could hold our breath. I did one of the longest and nearly killed myself, but that's me when someone sets me a challenge. Later on I wanted to be a synchronised swimmer like the girls in the Olympics on TV, and my friends and I copied their moves. We did elegant dives and backflips and I'd swirl around and twirl with my legs like when you make a whirlpool. I'd do it for hours, like dancing in the water. That's what I enjoyed more than the mechanics of swimming.

I was in the Girl Guides and one day we went to the pool from nine in the morning till closing time. We swam and swam and swam and at the end of the day I couldn't see for the chlorine. I had to go up and get a badge and I was going, 'I can't see. I've got this chlorine in my eyes.' I was burnt to a berry and everything was a fog but I managed to get up the stairs hanging on to the other girls' hands.

You could hire the pool out for birthday parties or engagement parties. That was really big in Murgon, and one time my sister-in-law and brother had a party for someone in the family's birthday. My mum was a bit of a card and she and my brother decided to have a race. My brother started at the deep end and Mum, who was very short, started where she could touch the bottom. My brother just beat her by a finger. He was six foot something but Mum wasn't a bad swimmer. I've got a beautiful photo of her in her togs when she was about 21.

Murgon had a very strong swimming club and they'd have a meet on a Wednesday night. I did one backstroke race. I was good at backstroke and then my sister said you've got to do one freestyle race. I did, but I wasn't interested in joining the club or training in the mornings and then back again in the afternoons. I could sprint for 50 metres so I'd be good in the relays at the school carnivals, but us Aboriginal girls were shy and swam with long tops over our togs and always had that constant drag. One of our teachers said, 'Why don't you take your tops off? You'll go faster.' One year I thought I might give it a shot. Me and a couple of the other Aboriginal girls stood on the blocks with our towels wrapped around us and, as we heard the gun fire for the start of the race, we dropped our towels and dived in. It was hilarious!

We didn't want to show our bodies. It was what we called *myall,* a term used back in the days of 'first settle' when Aborigines were called 'Myalls' by the white superiors. It was a word that carried a feeling of shame. That was handed down through the generations and it was ingrained in us not to dress in a provocative manner. It goes way back to the Cherbourg mission where my mother was born and where her mother had been taken in 1910 after being stolen from her Gunggari homelands of Mitchell in central Queensland. At the mission, the rules were handed down from the superintendent and my old people weren't allowed to look people in the eye or have an opinion or a voice. Their lives were governed by rules about how they dressed and behaved and they weren't considered beautiful. So that passed down to us and then it became us pulling ourselves down – like don't show off or 'big note'.

The Murgon Pool gave us freedom. We trusted the place. We relied on each other when we were there – all us kids from the five blackfella families in town. When our oldies went to the Sunday afternoon sessions at the pub, they'd send us to the pool. We knew we had the responsibility of looking after the younger ones and if one of us did have a dollar we'd make a bucket of hot chips go a long way. At the end of the day, there'd always be a big mob of us leaving. We'd walk home down the main drag towards the edge of town where we all lived. Families would peel off – the Renoufs first at the corner of Lamb and Palmer Streets, then the Leedies up the hill to the right at Perkins Street and then me and the Stanleys to the left. Perkins Street was the last street in town. We all headed inside, starving after another great day at the pool.

JAN CORNALL

Wrestling with boys in Rochester

When Jan Cornall was growing up in country towns in northern and western Victoria in the 1950s and 60s, she swam in creeks, rivers, waterholes, irrigation channels, lakes and mountain streams. But the place where she had the most fun was the local chlorine pool in Rochester, a small country town on the Campaspe River, where she was a top performer, executing an inward-pike off the diving board.

F our years after I was born in Melbourne in 1950, we moved to Shepparton, a northern Victorian town on the Goulburn River, so that my father could take up a teaching position at the high school there. Both my parents were teachers and every three or four years we moved to a new country town. When I was seven we moved south from Shepparton to Seymour, also on the Goulburn River.

Seymour was where my father taught me to swim, in a small creek with dark brown, brackish water that was part of the Goulburn River system. He showed me how to do a torpedo and to kick my legs and then he pushed me off. I glided over to the other side where someone was standing in this narrow waterhole. Then he showed me how to bring my arms over and after a few practices I'm pretty sure I learned to swim in that first session.

The big, wide and fast-flowing Goulburn River was at the end of our street in Seymour and on the side of the river were these timber baths. They were a wooden structure with steps leading down into the water. There was no entry fee or anything like that. My older brother Pip and I used to sit up on the bank of the river and then wander down for a dip. I have a memory of races being held in those river baths that were about 25 or 33 yards long, and the beautiful fragrance of the eucalypts along the river in the heat of the summer sun. The river water was always very dark and quite cold because it came down from the mountain. If you opened your eyes under water you couldn't see anything.

After we'd played around in the baths for a while, we'd get more adventurous and swim across the river to a little island. Pip was four years older than me and a very strong swimmer. I became a strong swimmer quite quickly after those lessons from Dad. Pip loved adventure and I would follow him anywhere. I remember him leading the way across the river. There was a quarry on the island and an old man lived in a shack there and we used to taunt him and throw pebbles at his house and he would threaten to chop our heads off. We'd spend all day down at the river and nobody worried where we were because we always came home eventually.

After about three years we moved on to the next town, St Arnaud in the Wimmera region of Victoria. At St Arnaud we swam in a former quarry and dam that had been used by a quartz reef mine in the late 1930s and had been transformed into a swimming pool by lining it with concrete. It was pretty big, with numerous diving structures, but the water could be quite murky and if your feet touched the bottom it felt quite creepy. My brother reckons we've probably got arsenic poisoning from swimming in the St Arnaud pool. All the school swimming carnivals were held there but it was never my favourite pool. I didn't find that place until we moved to the next town – Rochester, where I started swimming in the town's chlorine pool.

Like the other towns we'd lived in, Rochester was on a river, only this time it was the Campaspe rather than the Goulburn. It was a small town of less than 3000 people and surrounded by dairy farms. We arrived there in early January 1962 or 63, before the school year started, and soon after I went to the Rochester pool. It was pretty nondescript but it had seven lanes and was Olympic-size, not 33 yards, which many country pools were in the 1950s and 60s. There was a high diamond-wire fence around it and a concrete brick entrance with a little office, shop and changing rooms, and large areas of grass around the wading pool and big pool. There was also a springboard and a diving tower that wasn't super high.

Rochester Pool was where I had lots of formative girl-boy experiences from those early teen years to 15. I'd go there for the whole day with my towel, special little lotions, my sunglasses, and I'd buy packets of chips or Twisties. I flirted with boys and one boy in particular who was from the wrong side of the tracks. He had a few teeth missing and for some reason I always tended to be attracted to those types of boys.

We had a lot of fun just horsing around – that's what you did at the swimming pool. You were going through puberty but all your physical contact with boys was bombing each other, wrestling with and dunking each other and sometimes lying close to each other on towels on the spiky grass. I don't think we did any pashing at the pool because it was too open and public, but we did play-fighting and wrestling and the boys would get erections. We had no idea what it was – there was no sex education, so you didn't quite understand what was happening to them, but you knew something was going on.

I did my bronze medallion at Rochester Pool and I remember having to swim fully clothed and rescue people in the pool. I also went to swimming training early in the mornings three times a week and did diving training as well. At the school carnivals I was the diving champion, performing in my favourite red Speedos. I loved the complete focus of diving – the run-up, bouncing for three, making your body streamlined like an arrow and entering the water at a certain spot, as well as trying to be graceful and make as little splash as possible. It was like shooting a gun and hitting a target. At the time I didn't really think about it but reflecting now there was an extreme level of focus and aiming to be right on point. And then you're down in the water and when you come up, people clap your performance. It was a performance with your body; I wasn't aware that was what I was doing when I was 14, but it's interesting that after I left school, I became a performer, singer and comedian on the stage, which is pretty similar to diving off a cliff.

I mainly dived off the high board, which was probably about three metres, but I drew the line at diving backwards. I was good at doing inward pike dives and somersaulting front-ways, but I just couldn't dive backwards. My coach tried to teach me, as I had potential, but I could never go to the next level of fancy somersault diving and so I eventually stopped. We were brought up to be winners and in the swimming races both my brother and I were champions. We went in everything and we'd go off and win a race and come back and dump the medals in Mum or Dad's lap and then race off again and win another one. When I stopped diving it was my first experience of giving up on something. It wasn't a nice experience. Inwardly I felt like a failure.

Eventually I went to the pictures with that boy with the missing teeth but it wasn't a lasting relationship and when I was 16 we had our final move to Alexandra. It also had a pool, which I went to from time to time and for school carnivals. It was pretty much the same design as Rochester but on a different block and facing a different way. The loudspeaker is my most prominent memory of that pool. It was always a woman's voice calling out over the PA: 'Bobby, it's time to go home – your dad's here,' or, 'Laura, I've told you once, I've told you twice, if you do that again, you'll have to go home.' You could hear these announcements all over town.

I didn't have the same relationship with the Alexandra pool as I did with the one at Rochy. I'd moved into a different bracket of flirting with older boys who'd already left school and had cars and licences. One night after our matric exams they took us water skiing under a full moon at Lake Eildon. That was far more exciting than swimming at the Alexandra pool. After I finished school in 1967, I went to Melbourne and that was the end of my relationship with all those small-town pools.

But the memories of those places are still very strong – the sweet smell of eucalypts by a river on a hot day and all those lovely mountain creeks and waterfall pools we swam in on our adventurous family trips on weekends. But the Rochester pool was the most fun. I felt a level of freedom and joy in being physical at that pool in those years between 13 and 15 before all the heavy-duty self-consciousness of adolescence kicked in. I still felt strong in my body and I didn't hide it as I wrestled with boys on the grass, raced in the pool or dived off the tower. That pool was the centre of everything when I was a kid and I can still hear the soundtrack – there's laughter, squealing and splashing and someone talking on the loudspeaker: 'Jan, it's time to go home now! Your dad's here.'

LEE FONTANINI

Growing up at Fonty's Pool

In the early 1920s, Lee Fontanini's grandfather Archimedes (Archie) Fontanini transformed the dam on his farm near the Western Australian town of Manjimup into a palatial freshwater pool complete with pontoon, diving board and a children's wading pool. For generations, Fonty's Pool was the local public swimming spot for the residents of the south-west timber and farming community. In 1955 when Lee was born on the family orchard, 200 metres from the pool, she followed previous generations of her family in spending all summer at Fonty's.

I was a very active child, and when I wasn't riding my horse or my bike, I was at Fonty's Pool. After I got off the school bus I'd be rushing home to get my bathers on and race down there. I was quite a bit younger than my older brothers and sister, so I mainly went there with a whole swag of cousins, especially with my cousin Stephen, who was the same age as me. We'd walk up the dirt road eating a chunk of bread and jam and when we got hungry we'd go home for food or go to the orchard and grab an apple or a plum.

Louie, my family's boxer dog, always came with us to the pool. If he got bored he'd pinch your towel and there'd be this trail of kids chasing him to get it back. He was a very cheeky dog and we all loved him. I can't remember learning to swim but like most other people in Manjimup, I attended the government swimming lessons at Fonty's Pool. I can only remember being able to swim at this lovely pool so close to our orchard property that was part of Pop and Nana's original farm.

Pop had a strong presence at the pool and everyone would come and say hello to Fonty – that's what all the locals called him. He sat in the same spot by the pool each day, behind a small bench next to a storeroom. He'd have a large bottle opener in his hand to open the Cottee's drinks he sold. The drinks weren't refrigerated so they were always a bit warm. The Passiona was my favourite, lovely and sweet. Pop loved to watch everyone having fun at the pool and people would come and sit with him while their kids played and swam. He may not have seen someone for five years but he always remembered them. He had a great memory.

When I arrived in the world in 1955, Pop had been in Australia for 51 years: 'a land of opportunity', he called it. He was born at a place called Giuncugnano near the Tuscan town of Lucca in central Italy in 1880; his family were subsistence farmers. When he was 12 he was orphaned and at 16 he went to France and found work on a farm, where he learned building and stone masonry skills. At 20 he did his mandatory three years in the Italian army and volunteered to serve in China, where the Boxer Rebellion had erupted. When he came home after the war, things were pretty grim in the area where he lived. He'd heard there were opportunities opening up in Australia, so he got on a boat and landed in Fremantle in Western Australia in 1904.

For the first few years he worked at a timber mill in Greenbushes, north of Bridgetown, and learned English and grew vegetables. When the government opened up land in the virgin forest area south of Bridgetown, he went there with a surveyor and selected 160 acres and bought an additional 300 acres. He sent for his brother Germano (Jack), who came out from Italy and secured 160 acres of land next door. Importantly, a stream ran through both properties.

Pop cleared the swamp to grow vegetables and also used part of this land to build a dam. A large karri tree was pulled across the creek and soil was built up around it to form a wall. This was the only dam around in those days, and his family and other people in the community used to swim there. In the early 1920s the locals asked my grandfather to turn his dam into a public pool and charge an entry fee, as there were no rivers near Manjimup where one could be built. This was the beginning of Fonty's Pool.

To make it more like a pool, he lined the bed of the creek with gravel and concreted around the sides. He didn't actually concrete the whole floor of the pool until 1961. It was almost an acre in size and held 18 million litres of fresh water, with a winter flow rate of 44 000 litres per hour. The water flowed into the pool from the creek through a 24-inch pipe and nine smaller pipes in the wall. There were three overflows. The water was clear and fresh but if you'd been in there for a long time you'd get cold, so to warm up we'd lie down on the hot concrete path alongside the pool. It was always a favourite thing to do. The water was usually warm on the top and cold on the bottom, but when there were lots of people in there it got stirred up and the cold water would come to the top.

Pop and his wife Lucy, who was from Austria, also created extensive lawns and beautiful gardens with ornamental flowering cherries, displays of hydrangeas, roses, viburnum and various creepers, as well as plum, pear, cherry and apple orchards. The pool was officially opened in 1925 and from then on it was the place to be in summer. It was where swimming lessons and school carnivals were held, and where my father's brother Charlie turned into a state swimmer.

When I was growing up in the 1960s, Fonty's Pool and gardens were still considered the showpiece of the south-west and tourists flocked there. Pop introduced trout to the pool and when the tourist buses arrived he'd put on a show. He'd go to the edge of the pool and throw bread to the trout. He had a long poplar stick to keep the ducks away while he was feeding the trout, but after he was finished he'd throw the ducks some bread.

My favourite spot at the pool was definitely the diving board. It wasn't like diving boards at other pools. It was made of karri wood and specially crafted at the Pemberton Timber Mill. It was a pretty solid plank that had been weathered, oiled and painted with a non-slip paint. It was elevated about seven feet above the water on two concrete pillars and there was a ladder up to it. The water was only about six feet deep under the diving board but we seemed to manage and didn't hit the bottom.

It didn't bounce as high as a regular springboard, so you quickly learned to take the right number of steps to get a really good lift to do a half-somersault dive. If you wanted to create a big splash when you did a bombie you had to get a decent run-up along the board. One year when I went to Canberra for a school excursion we spent an afternoon at the Canberra Olympic Pool, which had a separate diving pool with a big tower and a springboard. I did the same run-up on the springboard as I did at Fonty's Pool, followed by a big bounce, and I got thrown all around the place. It had so much more spring than the karri plank at home. We had great fun on Fonty's board doing backflips, horsies and bombies and sometimes we used to fight on the board. We'd push each other aside to get to the front and people would end up toppling into the water.

The school swimming carnivals at the pool were fantastic and everyone was always excited when the big day arrived. The only thing I wasn't happy about was that I had to go to school on the bus and then come back to the pool with the rest of the school. The old cork swimming ropes would be connected and six lanes set up in an area that was 55 yards and we'd all gather on the lawn in our house teams of red, yellow, blue and green. I always did well in the swimming events and in the diving because I spent so much time on the board and knew it better than anyone else. My sister also broke quite a few swimming records and used to win school trophies.

In 1971, when I was 15, Pop was awarded a gold medal from the Chamber of Commerce in Lucca for gaining distinction in his new country and being a worthy ambassador for his homeland. A reporter who asked him how he felt about getting the award recorded his response that, 'He was human and enjoyed some flattery about the pool but the enjoyment he has had from his work has been more rewarding.' The year before, he received an MBE honouring his contribution to the community and tourist industry.

While he was the driver behind the pool and the beautiful grounds, I don't think he would have achieved what he did without the help and support of his wife Lucy. Pop lived till he was 102 but Nana died when she was 74 in 1954, the year before I was born. I'm sad I never met her, as from stories people have told me she was an amazing, hardworking woman who was integral to creating the farm and the pool from scratch, as well as bringing up five children. I'm sure Pop would have been proud of what they did, but he would never have said that out aloud to anyone. His satisfaction came from watching people having fun.

Fonty's Pool has always been part of my life and it still astounds me how a man from Italy who came to Australia with no English and almost no money created such an amazing asset for the community. It's no longer in the family but the present owners have done an absolutely fantastic job of improving the facilities while retaining the pool and the original building. And the wonderful thing is that I still live 200 metres from the pool in my family's original home, so whenever I feel nostalgic I just wander down the road and sit by the water, just like Pop did.

MERRICK WATTS

Disneyland in Broken Hill

Merrick Watts lived in the same house in the leafy
Melbourne suburb of Eltham from the time he
was born in November 1973 until he left home in
the early 1990s. As a child he swam in the family's
backyard pool, had lessons at the local indoor
pool, and skylarked with his mates in a tributary of
the Yarra River near his home. But none of these
swimming spots left their mark on his memory like
South Broken Hill's Alma Olympic Pool in outback
New South Wales.

From the time I was born, Broken Hill was a huge
part of my life. Mum and Dad and my older brother
Beechleigh and I used to go there in the holidays at least
once a year, usually twice, sometimes three times, and
stay with Mum's parents in the miner's cottage in South
Broken Hill where she grew up. When I was older I'd go
up on my own on the Greyhound bus or sometimes catch
the train to Mildura and then the bus. Broken Hill was

more than 800 kilometres from Melbourne, so it took me all day and into the night to get there.

Pop was a BHP miner and Nana was a teacher. They were a super proletarian, working-class couple. Nana's name was Alma, and when I was little I thought South Broken Hill's Alma Olympic Pool was named after her. She died when I was five, but Pop kept going till he was 89, even though he had broken his back falling down a mineshaft and had to have 12 operations. He was made of tough stuff, like most people in Broken Hill.

In the 1970s and 80s I had a few swims in the City Pool at North Broken Hill, which was awesome, but the Alma Pool at South Broken Hill was the main one. It was just up the road from Pop's house and that's where I used to swim all the time. Every day. All day.

The Alma Pool was like a time capsule, with old-school turnstiles and a 1960s façade. It had an Olympic-size pool and a kiddies' wading pool. The big pool was surrounded by large areas of concrete and we were always looking for wet patches to step on, otherwise we'd burn our feet. Beyond the concrete was the immaculately kept lawn, and near the fence-line were a few gum trees.

It cost five cents for kids and 20 cents for adults and when we got to the entrance, I couldn't wait to get inside. I'd be breaking my neck, and once I was through the turnstiles I'd run to our little perch on the grass at the shallow end of the big pool. That's where we'd leave our towels. When we first went to the pool with our parents we sat there, as it was more of a family area close to the kiddies' pool, and we kept it going. There was a bit of shade there too, which was important because if you didn't have shade on one of those 40-degree days, you'd cook. The local youth sat on the opposite side to us and smoked and swore.

My earliest memories are of the kiddie pool, not the big pool. Mum has a photo of my brother and me in the kiddie pool when I'm two and two months (she always put the date on the back of the photos) and Beechleigh's drinking the water out of the little fountain. You weren't meant to drink the water but my brother clearly thought he was a labrador. The pool was very shallow, curved like a semi-kidney shape, and there was no shade. I loved being in that little pool because the water was cold, you could get away from the heat and you could play for hours. At that stage our parents would have been there keeping a passive eye on us. They were lizards so they were probably sunbaking.

There's another photo of my brother and me in the kiddie pool when I'm six or seven and I am forcing him underwater. We're holding each other's arms and fighting like gladiators. I was always very strong and a strong swimmer. Mum and Dad had us taught to swim early and were really into making sure we could swim well, so by the time I was about four I'd moved on to the big pool where there was a diving board and a slippery slide. I played around the steps, skirting around the edges and the ladders, and by the time I was five I was on my own in that pool. Then I progressed further up the deep end, which got deep fairly quickly because they used to have a diving tower. I only went back to the little pool to punch up my brother.

Once my brother and I could swim well, when we were about seven or eight, we were allowed to go to the pool on our own. Pop had these stand-up fans and a water evaporator which he ran at night, and big trees over one side of the house to ward off the western sun, but we'd always wake up in the morning with the heat. The minute we felt it, we'd be up and out of the canvas camp beds we slept on in Pop's lounge room, have breakfast, then out the door. We would be given a few dollars and our parents didn't see us until dusk – except on the really hot days when we came home for lunch and had a 'Stral-ian' sandwich with Devon – or fritz, as Pop called it.

We had five cousins in Broken Hill and we'd always check if they wanted to come to the pool. They lived not far from Pop in South Broken Hill, which was always regarded as the shittier side of town, with a massive hill of mine waste separating it from the north side. Our cous-ins were not as wild as my brother and me, and when they got to the pool they'd be covered in sunscreen as they had fairer skin. On stinking hot days our parents put sun-screen on us, but if it was sub-30 degrees we didn't wear it. We had olive skin and within days of being at the pool we'd be as brown as berries.

We spent a lot of time with our cousins, but they weren't as delighted by the pool as my brother and me. For us it was like a mini-Disneyland – our first experience of a theme park. The pool had a diving board, a slide, open space and it was not as policed as city pools were. Back then at the South Broken Hill pool you had to get pretty loose to be sanctioned by the manager. There were no lifeguards, so you could run around and kick a ball, play chasings and wrestle on the lawn. As long as you weren't being too much of a problem you could cut it pretty sick and there was so much to do. We never got bored.

One of the games we used to do all the time was get 10- or 20-cent pieces and throw them in and dive for them. It was a very deep pool, built to cater for a diving tower, so if a coin made it to the bottom before we grabbed it, we had to dive down four metres. I could handle the pressure but I think it perforated my eardrums because I've got swimmer's ear something chronic.

The other trick was to swim the length underwater. One time I got further than that and did one and a half laps. I dived off the blocks, which gave me a bit of a head start, and swam underwater on the bottom like a stingray. The rule was you couldn't break the surface. At the end I tumble-turned and made it back to the ladder in the centre. When I came up everyone was looking at me – the entire pool. Dad saw me, and when I got out of the water, the look on my old man's face was a really strange combination of pride and horror, because when I came up I was very, very close to being in a bad way. I was dizzy and nearly asphyxiated myself. There's a lot of things that nearly killed me when I was a youth and that was one of them.

The big thing was the bombing comp. We'd get up on the blocks and absolutely throw ourselves into doing a bomb and see who could make the biggest splash. We'd do the different styles – the horsey holding one leg and the double banger with both legs and then, depending on the angle of entry, everyone made different concussive sounds when they struck the water. When you went under there was this delay and then there was this boom and the water would fly up and you'd hear the cavitation. We'd never see our own bombs but we'd hear the cavitation and be able to say, 'Oh that's good. I've nailed that.' Then you'd get up as quickly as you could and look to your cousins or your brother and they'd give you the thumbs-up, or they'd say 'That was good!'

There was no end to the games we made up and played. We'd throw an object in the water and the first person to get it won; we'd get all the paddle-pop sticks together and make little rafts and sail them in the water. When we got bored with a game we'd run around the lawn and wrestle and fight each other and when we got itchy from the grass we'd get back in the water.

At some stage we'd have to go into the change rooms but we didn't want to go there because of paedos. We didn't know what a paedophile was, but in the 1970s and 80s we were shown stranger danger videos at primary school and it was the period when Mr Baldy and Mr Stinky were on the loose in Melbourne. They were murderers, rapists and paedophiles and we were paranoid that they'd be in the change rooms. If I had to go to the toilet I'd usually go with my brother or a cousin and pee and get out as fast as I could. There was absolutely nothing going on in there. There was never anybody in there but we felt like we were going into a spider's nest.

The manager always blared classic hits radio through the loudspeakers so everyone just had to listen to it. I remember very distinctly hearing The Police and The Cars and a whole lot of songs of the time that were hits when I was a boy. And then there were the treats at the pool that we weren't allowed to have when we were at home. We'd get a bag of mixed lollies with sherbet sticks, a Paddle-Pop or a cola, lemonade or raspberry icy pole. My favourite was a vanilla ice cream with raspberry jelly dimples on the outside. I can't remember its name but I'm pretty sure it was made by Great North, a South Australian company. Broken Hill was very close to South Australia so a lot of products came from there.

When I saw my first icy pole stick made out of plastic, I thought, *What is that?* It was like a little Tetris and I thought, *This is the future.* And the first time I saw a microwave pizza in my life was at the South Broken Hill pool. My dad got one for lunch and we were like, *What?*

'How are you eating pizza from the pool, Dad?'

'I went to the shop.'

'But it's pizza, Dad. How did they make it hot?'

'In the microwave.'

And I'm like, *What?* It blew my mind.

We didn't really mix with the locals. They wore South Australian Football League footy shorts to the pool, and as teenagers my brother and I wore Quiksilver or Rip Curl board shorts, which stuck out like dog's balls. That was probably enough to cause some trouble in Broken Hill; they didn't like showy people or outsiders. I had a few scraps – my brother was a much calmer soul. I loved verbally baiting the locals because I knew I could back it up physically. I baited them just for fun – not menacingly – but just because I enjoyed the sport of it. My father used to do it in pubs in Broken Hill and my mum said she was always astonished that he never got beaten up, because he was an advertising executive from Brighton in Melbourne who drove a Mercedes and he could be a wanker. What saved him was that he was married to the daughter of a local miner.

A few times I got into actual fights at the pool and the manager would come out and break them up. Usually, because we were out-of-towners, he assumed the local kids had tried to lynch me, so they'd be kicked out. From the other side of the fence they'd say they were going to get me and I'd say, 'Well, that's fine because I'm staying here till my parents come and pick me up, so you just wait on that side of the fence.' And I'd wait and hope they'd think my parents *were* coming to pick me up because they weren't. Then I'd have to get my cousins to go back to Pop's place and get my dad to come in the car and pick me up, otherwise I was going to get totally destroyed. I could be a dickhead!

So, I had a couple of little stoushes there but generally the pool was like a waterhole somewhere in Africa where you've got all these different species that have to find a harmonious moment because the heat is their enemy. It was like when you see animals shoulder to shoulder that wouldn't normally be side by side. The tiger thinks, *Do I want to kill that gazelle? Or do I just want to get a drink?* And he decides, *Let's have a drink, thanks!* Most of the time on those really hot days there wouldn't be any problems at the pool as everyone was just so glad to have that option of cool water. If you lived in the city you had tons of options, but in Broken Hill, the pool was the only place to cool down.

Water was always scarce in Broken Hill and when there was a drought we were never allowed to have a shower on our own. We'd have to shower in pairs and my pop would be so strict and say, 'You've got one minute.' And you'd never have hot water because it was so hot. There always seemed to be water restrictions, so no one could play under a hose or run through a sprinkler, and it was a rare treat when we'd go to our cousins' and play slip and slide.

The first time I started to see the opposite sex in a slightly different way was at the South Broken Hill pool. Before, they were potentially an obstacle to getting on the slide, and then all of a sudden I'm okay that they go on the slide before me. But I never hooked up with a girl from Broken Hill. There were certainly a few times I would have liked to but they were too foreign and I didn't know how to speak to them. We spoke to them with this kind of city mentality and they thought we were fucking wankers. I was the worst and I think for a lot of them that was the charm, because I was extremely confident – overly confident.

The first Aboriginal kid I saw was at that pool. There wasn't a huge Aboriginal population in Broken Hill and being from the outer suburbs of Melbourne I didn't meet or see Aboriginal people. At the pool they just played like the rest of us and we played with them, and we didn't give it any thought. I do remember a sense of separation though but again, going back to the water hole analogy, in that space people couldn't afford to be bigoted or cruel for a minute, it was simply too hot.

The last time I went to the South Broken Hill pool was in my late teens or early twenties. I took my American girlfriend with me and stayed at Pop's place. She loved the desert and thought Broken Hill was so different from anywhere else. It was cool to have somebody to share it with. After Pop died I stopped going to the 'Hill' until a few years ago when I took my wife and children there. I showed them everything. Mum and Pop's old tin house, the milk bar, the pubs, the memorial to the miners, but I couldn't go past the pool. It was just so sad and heart-breaking that something I loved so much as a child was just dirt now – the council closed it down in 2002 because it was leaking water, and later it was demolished. When I told my mum she said, 'Well, that's kind of Broken Hill's story. It's boom and bust.' The population has almost halved since the 70s and now it's all fly-in-fly-out workers on the mines and they don't make towns.

The South Broken Hill pool is so heavily imprinted on me because when I went there I had nothing but fun and I had so much freedom. The sun was always out and it was warm on my skin. There was always cool water to play in and everyone was in a good mood. Every single day when we were at Pop's house I looked forward to going to the pool, and those weeks each summer are my earliest, fondest, most vivid memories of childhood. I still have dreams about the place because it was so heavily anchored in what I loved more than any other time. It was the greatest place on earth when I was a kid!

Biographical notes

David Bartlett

David Bartlett is a former premier of Tasmania and Labor MP for the seat of Denison in the Tasmanian House of Assembly from 2004 to 2011. He is currently a keynote speaker on innovation through technology, the president of the Hobart Chargers basketball club, and for four years chaired the Brave Foundation, a charity that equips teenage parents with resources and opportunities for education. In 1987 he was reunited with his birth mother, and later with his father. In 2014 when his portrait was unveiled in the Tasmanian Parliament, both his birth parents and his foster parents were present. A cold-water enthusiast, he swims with a group of hardy souls in Hobart's Derwent River throughout the winter. He lives in Hobart with his wife Larissa and their two children.

Bryan Brown

Bryan Brown is an Australian actor and producer who has performed in more than 80 film, television and theatre productions, including *Breaker Morant*, *The Thorn Birds* and *Sweet Country*. Since establishing New Town

Films in 1983, he has produced many projects, including *Palm Beach*, released in 2019 and directed by his wife Rachel Ward. Over the years he has received numerous accolades including the 2018 Longford Lyell Award from the Australian Academy of Cinema and Television Arts (AACTA), recognising his outstanding contribution to Australia's screen culture. He was also honoured in 2013 when the Bryan Brown Theatre and Function Centre in Bankstown was named after him. A keen swimmer since his Bankstown Baths days, he loves a dip in the ocean and swimming laps at his local pool.

Lizzie Buckmaster Dove

Since graduating with a Bachelor of Fine Arts from the University of New South Wales in 1993, Lizzie Buckmaster Dove has exhibited her collages, works on paper, photography, installations and found-object art in more than 30 group and solo exhibitions. Inspired by nature and her local area, sea pools featured in her 2013 installation *Pool: The Alchemy of Blue*, made from small, sea-worn fragments of blue-painted concrete eroded from the Coledale ocean pool, and *A Year of Walking*, photographs celebrating the Illawarra's unique history of ocean pools. Her latest creative project is a series of poems accompanying Wollongong Art Gallery's 2018–19 *Summer Love* exhibition. Currently focusing on writing, Lizzie swims regularly at her local Coledale ocean pool with her husband and three children.

Richard Chmielewski

Richard Chmielewski enjoyed every minute of the 28 years he spent in the Royal Australian Air Force (RAAF),which he joined in 1977 aged 16. Working as an aircraft technician, his RAAF career gave him opportunities to travel overseas, live in different parts of Australia and complete a Masters in Aviation Management. After leaving the air force he held various roles at a company that recycled waste from wine-making into products such as high-grade ethanol, and currently works in Adelaide's fuel storage industry. A father of three adult children, he has a passion for motorcycling and gets pleasure from gardening and being a home-handyman. He is a life-long swimmer with a favourite spot, the Edithburgh Tidal Pool on the Yorke Peninsula, where he enjoys glimpsing the sunrise as he does laps at dawn.

Ellen Connor

Ellen Connor spent her childhood in the inner Melbourne suburbs of Northcote, Brunswick and Collingwood. When she left school, she completed studies in event management and a TAFE course in childcare, and worked in childcare for a number of years. She is currently undertaking a diploma of community services, is involved in local Labor politics and the ACTU's Change the Rules campaign for pay rises. Since moving to Geelong with her family eight years ago, the Eastern Beach Swimming Enclosure has become a favourite place to take her two daughters for a swim. She still enjoys playing the flute, is a member of Geelong Trades Hall Choir, and when she's back in Melbourne she drops into Fitzroy Pool for a swim.

Priya Cooper

Priya Cooper is one of the most successful athletes in Australian swimming history. A competitor in the Paralympics at Barcelona in 1992, Atlanta in 1996 and Sydney in 2000, she has won nine gold, three silver and four bronze medals. She was co-captain of the Australian team at the 1996 Atlanta Paralympics and at the Sydney 2000 games, and carried the Australian flag at the closing ceremonies of the 1992 and 1996 Paralympics. She has received numerous awards including a Medal of the Order of Australia. In October 2015 she became the fourth Paralympian to be inducted into the Sport Australia Hall of Fame. She holds a degree in health promotion and media from Perth's Curtin University and with her husband, fellow Paralympian Rodney Bonsack, runs a motivational business. Based in Perth, she has two children and one stepson.

Jan Cornall

Jan Cornall is a writer and performer who was a leader in the women's comedy and cabaret resurgence of the early 1980s. She was a founding member of the Tribe experimental theatre group in 1968 and in the late 1970s was writer in residence at Melbourne's Pram Factory. She has written more than 15 plays and musicals, a feature film, a novel, *Take Me to Paradise*, and *Archipelago: Love Songs to Indonesia*, a collection of poems and stories. She has an MA in cultural and creative practice and for nearly two decades has mentored writers and taught creative writing in Australia and Asia. She lives in Sydney, where her favourite pool is the Bronte Baths, a place she often took her two children to swim when they were small.

Trent Dalton

Trent Dalton is a staff writer for the *Weekend Australian Magazine* and former assistant editor of the *Courier Mail*. He's a two-time Walkley Award winner for Excellence in Journalism, a four-time winner of the Kennedy Award for Excellence in NSW Journalism, and a four-time winner of the national News Awards Features Journalist of the Year. His first novel, *Boy Swallows Universe*, published by HarperCollins in 2018, has sold more than 100 000 copies in Australia and has been published in the UK, the US and translated into 12 languages. In 2019, *Boy Swallows Universe* took out more than seven awards, including the Australian Book Industry's Literary Fiction Book of the Year. He lives in Brisbane with his wife Fiona and two daughters in a house with a backyard pool.

Tony Doherty

During Tony Doherty's more than 50 years as a Catholic priest, he has been a hospital chaplain, adult educator, writer, media commentator and parish priest. In 1995 he coordinated the visit of Pope John Paul II to Sydney for the beatification of Mary Mackillop, and later was appointed Dean of St Mary's Cathedral, during which time the two cathedral spires were completed to the original design of 1865. In 2012 he received an Order of Australia and in 2017 he published the book *The Attachment: Letters from a most unlikely friendship* with fellow writer Ailsa Piper. Now 85, he continues a lifetime habit of swimming daily in the harbour pool of Sydney's Nielsen Park.

Diane Fingleton

Diane Fingleton is a former Queensland Chief Magistrate who was instrumental in bringing about the implementation of the Murri Court and leading an apology to Indigenous Australians for past injustices perpetrated by the Queensland legal system. Other roles include working for Bill Hayden, the Minister for Social Security in the Whitlam Government, and as a solicitor for community legal services. In 2003 her brother Tony's film *Swimming Upstream*, documenting her family's story, was released. Around this time she began the biggest battle of her life when a disgruntled employee took her to court. Always resilient but still recovering from the ordeal, Diane lives in Brisbane with her husband John and continues to love to swim.

Lee Fontanini

After completing her nursing training at Manjimup's Warren District Hospital, Lee Fontanini worked and travelled throughout her home state of Western Australia.

She spent 12 years at the Derby Regional Hospital in the Kimberley region, which gave her the opportunity to get to know the local Indigenous people and fall in love with that extraordinary ancient landscape. Since then she has regarded the Kimberley as her second home, after the Karri country in the south-west where she grew up and now lives. She is a keen photographer, bird-watcher and nature-lover with a passion for the environment, and while she considers the waterholes in the Kimberley amazing places, Fonty's Pool will always be her favourite swimming spot.

Shane Gould

A water-lover from an early age, by the time Shane Gould was 14 she was breaking New South Wales and Australian records. At 15 she won five individual medals at the 1972 Munich Olympic Games, and to date she is the only swimmer in history to hold all freestyle event records and the 200-metres individual medley at the same time. Since retiring from competitive swimming in 1973, she has raised four children and completed two Masters degrees – one on the social functions of public swimming pools. In 2019 she completed a PhD exploring the culture of swimming in Australia and won *Australian Survivor*: *Champions vs Contenders*, screened in 2018 on Channel Ten. She lives in Bicheno, Tasmania, with her husband, Milton Nelms, and swims most mornings with the local ocean swimming group.

Ashley Hay

Ashley Hay is the author of four non-fiction books and three novels, including the award-winning *The Railwayman's Wife*, set in Thirroul, just south of her home town of Austinmer. In 2014 that novel won the People's Choice Award at the New South Wales Premier's Literary Awards and received the Foundation for Australian Literary Studies' Colin Roderick Award. In 2016 her essay 'The Forest at the Edge of Time' won the Bragg/UNSW Press Prize for Science Writing. Her essays, science writing, short stories, reviews and articles have appeared in anthologies, journals and newspapers in Australia and internationally, and in 2018 she was appointed editor of the *Griffith Review*, an Australian quarterly of ideas and literary writing. She lives in Brisbane but regularly returns to Austinmer.

Linda Kennedy

Linda Kennedy spent the first three years of her life in a house without electricity or running water at Stenhouse Bay at the bottom of South Australia's Yorke Peninsula, where her father worked in the gypsum mine. For the rest of her childhood she lived in Adelaide. Since becoming a registered nurse in the early 1980s, she has largely worked in aged care. She is a mother of three and grandmother of seven. Throughout her life she has continued her childhood passion of collecting driftwood and shells, and in more recent times has turned them into works of art. She lives in Adelaide with her partner Rick but enjoys spending time at their holiday home at Edithburgh on the Yorke Peninsula, not far from her favourite swimming spot, the Hollywood Pool.

Merv Knowles

Merv Knowles was a senior Commonwealth public servant and Australian trade commissioner to Greece, Indonesia and Taiwan. Apart from two years in the Australian Army during World War II, and when his work took him overseas and interstate, he has been a regular morning swimmer at Canberra's Manuka Pool. When he retired in 1983, he became a member of the Coneheads, a group of former public servants who swim laps each morning and gather at the deep end steps for philosophical discussions. A former president of the Canberra and District Historical Society and Apex and Rotary office bearer, he has been married to his wife Beth since 1946. In June 2019 he turned 97, and until recently was still swimming laps each morning at his second home, Manuka Pool.

Daniel Kowalski

Daniel Kowalski is an Olympic swimmer who in 1996 at the Atlanta Olympics was the first man in 92 years to win medals in the 200, 400 and 1500 metres freestyle events at one Olympic Games. He also had success at four world swimming championships. At the 2000 Olympics in Sydney he was part of the gold-medal-winning squad in the 4 × 200-metres freestyle relay. Since retiring in 2002, he has held roles in sports administration and athlete advocacy and is currently Olympian Services Manager at the Australian Olympic Committee. An ambassador for mental health organisation Beyond Blue, he is passionate about supporting LGBTI athletes and working to change homophobic attitudes in sport. He lives in Sydney and when his shoulders, which have undergone four reconstructions, allow, he enjoys swimming at the Andrew Boy Charlton Pool.

Jo-Anne Larter

Jo-Anne Larter has spent many years working in the airline and travel industries throughout Australia and overseas. She has also been involved in horseracing and has run a number of businesses, including Larter's Cellars. In 2016 she returned to her home town of Launceston and since then has been working with her father Barry on his chairlift business at Cataract Gorge, where she gets to spend every day in paradise. A dog lover and owner of two Rhodesian Ridgebacks, she is a keen walker, and in summer swims every lunchtime at the First Basin Pool, just like she did when she was a kid.

Laurie Lawrence

Since 1966 Laurie Lawrence has taught thousands of children to swim, progressed them through junior squads and produced state, national, Commonwealth, world and Olympic champions, including Stephen Holland, Tracey Wickham, Duncan Armstrong and Jon Sieben. He was one of the coaches of the Australian Olympic swimming team for the Los Angeles games in 1984, Seoul in 1988 and Barcelona in 1992, and continued his involvement for four more Olympics, where his role was to unite, inspire and motivate the team. A world leader in teaching babies to swim, in 1998 he created the *Kids Alive – Do the Five* water safety program in response to a spate of pre-school drownings. Still committed and passionate about teaching children of all ages to love water and be safe, he lives on the Gold Coast with his wife Jocelyn.

Tess Lea

Tess Lea is a writer, doctor of philosophy and anthropologist who specialises in the anthropology of policy in the areas of infrastructure inequalities, housing, health, education and creative industries. She was the inaugural director of the School for Social Policy and Research at Darwin's Charles Darwin University, and is currently associate professor in the Department of Gender and Cultural Studies at the University of Sydney. A born and bred Darwinite, she is the author of *Darwin*, one of a series of books on Australian cities, and *Bureaucrats and Bleeding Hearts: Indigenous Health in Northern Australia,* both published by NewSouth. A dog lover, swimmer and mother, since moving to Sydney in 2008 she has become an ocean enthusiast and enjoys swimming between Shelley Beach and Manly on summer weekends.

John McSweeney

John McSweeney had a career in education as a primary teacher at state schools in Melbourne and regional Victoria, and 12 years teaching hearing impaired students across all school sectors. In 1979 he graduated as a naturopath and osteopath from the Southern School of Natural Therapies, and since then has run his own business from his Brighton home. A veteran of 15 Melbourne marathons, he has also competed in 21 Lorne Pier to Pub ocean swims. In his spare time he teaches adults to swim, and in recent years has become a Brighton Baths Iceberger, swimming through the winter months. On alternate days he does laps at the Melbourne Sports and Aquatic Centre by Albert Park, where he occasionally re-enacts a graceful dive from his youth.

Kim Mettam

Kim Mettam grew up on the border of Scarborough and Wembley Downs in Perth. He completed a degree in business at Curtin University and holds a Masters in industrial relations from the University of Western Australia. During his career in management for British and American multinational companies, he specialised in mentoring individuals and helping start-up companies get established. He has a passion for history and enjoyed discovering his family's link to a Viking with the Danish name for sea-wolf, giving the Mettam family an ancient link to the sea. He lives in Perth with his wife Yvonne, and when their two children were little, they continued the family tradition of learning to swim and snorkel at Mettam's Pool.

Yusra Metwally

Yusra Metwally is a policy adviser, lawyer and opinion writer with a passion for advocacy and social justice. Since graduating from university she has worked in policy and legal roles in the public and community sector. In 2017 she founded Swim Sisters to inspire women of all backgrounds, walks of life, fitness levels, shapes and sizes to go for a swim. Since forming Swim Sisters, she has made groundbreaking connections with surf lifesaving clubs and swimming schools to support women in the group to develop their open-water and pool swimming skills. A keen cyclist, Yusra lives in western Sydney with her husband and baby son, who she is hoping will become a water baby just like his mum.

Leah Purcell

Leah Purcell is an award-winning actor, writer and director and a proud Goa-Gunggari-Wakka Wakka Murri woman, who has appeared in countless theatre roles and on the big and small screen. Her credits include her semi-autobiographical play *Box the Pony*, *Black Chicks Talking*, *Lantana*, *Jindabyne*, *Redfern Now*, *Cleverman*, *Janet King* and *Wentworth*. In 2017 her theatre adaption of Henry Lawson's *The Drover's Wife* received multiple awards, including the Gold AWGIE at the annual Australian Writers' Guild awards, and it is currently being made into a film, a TV series and a novel. She lives in Sydney with her partner Bain Stewart, her daughter and two grandsons, but regularly returns to see friends and family in Murgon, where she loves to sit by the creek and swim in the Murgon Jubilee Pool.

Lily Sisa

After completing a business degree at Charles Sturt University in Bathurst, Lily Sisa returned home to Lightning Ridge and for eight years managed the Black Opal Motel. She has also worked as a personal assistant for her father's business and since 2012 has been president of the Lightning Ridge Olympic Swimming Pool Association. This voluntary role involves managing the sports and aquatic complex and ensuring it is well-maintained for the benefit of the local community and visitors to the town. A committee member for the local diving club and pony club, she enjoys travelling, reading, swimming and spending quality time with family and friends, including her fellow pool fundraisers from nearly 30 years ago, who all still live in Lighting Ridge and the surrounding opal fields.

Mick Thomas

Mick Thomas is best known as the lead singer of the iconic folk-rock band Weddings Parties Anything, which he formed in Melbourne in 1984. The group toured nationally and internationally, produced well-known songs like 'Father's Day' and 'Monday Experts', and won four ARIA music awards before disbanding in 1998. Mick's music has appeared on the soundtracks of more than eight ABC and SBS short films and documentaries. He has written a country rock opera, *Over in the West*, performed at Melbourne's Playbox Theatre, and the musical scores for several plays. Since 2011 he has toured and recorded with his new band, Mick Thomas and the Roving Commission. He lives in Melbourne with his wife Jen Huntly and their daughter, and is a regular swimmer at the Fitzroy, Collingwood and Richmond pools.

Diane Vukelic

After completing university studies in economics in Perth and Japan, Diane Vukelic has worked in project and business management across the corporate and education sectors. She is currently project manager with Childfund Australia, the official charity for the 2019 Japan Rugby World Cup, and is a director of the Australia–Japan Society of New South Wales. In 2017 she co-founded Celebrating Women in Japan, a social action initiative recognising women in Japan. She was part of a group that helped guarantee the National Art School's future in 2019, and was involved in saving Sydney's Andrew Boy Charlton Pool from closing in the 1990s. Drawn to water, she is a keen sailor and a director of the Woollahra Sailing Club. She lives in Sydney with her husband and their two teenage children, who enjoy their local swimming spot, Prince Alfred Park Pool.

Merrick Watts

For more than 20 years Merrick Watts was one half of the Merrick and Rosso comedy radio duo with Tim Ross; the two met on the stand-up circuit in Melbourne in the mid-1990s. In recent years Merrick has carved a new course as a solo performer with his 2017 stand-up comedy show *Man of the Hour*, as well as in acting roles on TV programs *The Hollowmen* and *Underbelly*, and as a comedian on *Thank God You're Here*, *The Project* and *Hughesy, We Have a Problem*. A self-described bogan and mad Collingwood AFL fan, he lives in a converted lolly factory in Sydney with his wife Georgie and enjoys joining his two children doing a bomb or two in their backyard pool.

Acknowledgements

First of all, I want to say a big thank you again to the 27 people in this book for telling me their 'memory pool' stories.

To Phillipa McGuinness for saying yes to my Twitter message asking her if she'd read the first eight chapters of the book, and for championing it to the wonderful team at NewSouth Publishing. Thanks also to Phillipa and to Emma Hutchinson for their enthusiasm and encouragement throughout the various stages of getting the book to publication. Special thanks to my editor Linda Funnell for her thoughtful review of the 28 stories in the book, and to Sandy Cull for her beautiful cover design.

To Bronwyn Birdsall, with whom I share a writing space at Writing NSW in Rozelle, I can't thank you enough for the chats, the walks around the grounds of Callan Park, the coffee breaks, and for being an astute sounding board. Thanks also to Felicity Jagavkar and Sarah Lambert, our top-floor neighbours at Writing NSW for your company, conversation and support, and to the staff at Writing NSW.

To my early readers, Jenny Power, Louisa Costa and Vanessa Weiss – your enthusiasm for the stories and

Acknowledgements

your perceptive comments encouraged me to keep going and gave the project momentum. To my gang of regular morning swimmers at Petersham's Fanny Durack Aquatic Centre, I appreciated the poolside chats, especially during the busy period of completing the interviews and stories.

A very big thank you to my family and friends, especially my husband Bruce, who has lived through the various stages of this book. I am grateful for his love and support, particularly during the intense phase of completing *The Memory Pool*, and for all those times he did a U-turn in a country town when I spotted a sign to the local swimming pool. Finally, I am eternally grateful to my parents, Barby and John Spruhan, for introducing me to the joys of water, swimming, the ocean and pools.